OBSESSIVE COMPULSIVE DISORDER

The Essential Guide

Joanna Jast

Obsessive-Compulsive Disorder – The Essential Guide is also available in accessible formats for people with any degree of visual impairment. The large print edition and eBook (with accessibility features enabled) are available from Need2Know. Please let us know if there are any special features you require and we will do our best to accommodate your needs.

First published in Great Britain in 2011 by
Need2Know
Remus House
Coltsfoot Drive
Peterborough
PE2 9BF
Telephone 01733 898103
Fax 01733 313524
www.need2knowbooks.co.uk

Contents

Introduction

Obsessive-compulsive disorder (OCD) is the fourth most common mental disorder after depression, drug and alcohol problems, and social phobia. It is believed that one in every 50 people suffers from OCD at some point in their life, which amounts to an army of around one million people in the UK alone.

There are a surprising number of famous people who have struggled with OCD in their lives. Examples include; English naturalist and the author of the *Theory of Evolution*, Charles Darwin; celebrity footballer David Beckham; Florence Nightingale and Howard Hughes – whose life and illness is so well captured by Leonardo DiCaprio in Martin Scorsese's film 'Aviator'.

So if you experience unpleasant, anxiety-provoking thoughts, despite your efforts to resist them (obsessions), and as a consequence you feel urges to perform certain acts repeatedly (compulsions), you are not alone.

OCD is time-consuming and causes of lot of stress to the sufferer. Tormenting thoughts and urges are the main source of anxiety, but the symptoms also impact on the person's family and professional life, creating more difficulties. OCD can be very disabling and have devastating effects on the person's work, social life and relationships. The World Health Organisation (WHO) has put it as tenth on their list of most disabling illnesses because of the loss of income and poor quality of life OCD is responsible for. In the worst case scenario, the life of an OCD sufferer may be completely overtaken by fighting intrusive thoughts and carrying out rituals. It is, however, important to remember that OCD is a treatable illness and can be overcome with appropriate help and support.

If you suffer from OCD, or care for someone who does, this book will improve your understanding of the illness and teach you how to recognise its symptoms. It will give you an overview of different treatment methods and advice on when, where and how to seek appropriate help and support. Armed with this knowledge and practical tips on what you can do to help yourself or your loved one to get better and stay well, you will be more confident in your battle against OCD.

'OCD is the fourth most common mental disorder. It is believed that one in every 50 people suffers from OCD at some point in their life.'

How to use this book

This book has been written with OCD sufferers and their carers in mind. Ideally, they will be able to use the guide together, to share understanding of the illness and advice on how to overcome the difficulties and speed up the recovery process. However, if for whatever reason, you are fighting OCD on your own, this book will help you to find support and will assist you on your journey of recovery and getting your life back on track.

The first part of this book (chapters 1 and 2) focuses on the illness itself, explaining the symptoms and providing information on what causes it. Chapters 3 and 4 explain what treatment methods and support are available, their effectiveness, how to access it, and what you need to consider while making your choice. The book also contains a special section for people who care for OCD sufferers (chapter 5) with advice on helpful techniques, and seeking support for themselves. As OCD happens to children too, chapter 6 is dedicated to young people and their struggles with obsessive thoughts, compulsions and rituals, as well as information on available treatment. Chapter 7 provides an overview of other mental disorders that often accompany OCD. Chapter 8 is dedicated to practical advice on living with OCD, coping with setbacks and relapses, and the rights of the sufferers. Chapter 9 focuses on staying well, moving on and going back to normal life.

The final section of the book contains a list of organisations and web resources that can provide more information and support for OCD sufferers and their carers.

Disclaimer

This book provides general information and advice on obsessive-compulsive disorder and is not intended to replace medical advice, but may be used alongside it. If you are concerned that you may be suffering from OCD, you should consult your health care professional as soon as possible.

The case studies in this book are purely fictional, but demonstrate posssible situations.

Chapter One

What is OCD?

Obsessive-compulsive disorder is a mental illness characterised by persistent, unwanted, unpleasant thoughts (obsessions), which cause a lot of anxiety; and repetitive, irrational urges to carry out acts aimed at reducing the anxiety or neutralising the obsessive thought (compulsions).

Obsessions and compulsions are distressing and time-consuming. Sufferers usually realise these symptoms are irrational and senseless, but they can't 'just stop them'. OCD is often called 'the secretive illness', as the feelings of embarrassment, guilt and shame related to the illness may prevent people from seeking help.

How common is it?

OCD is one of the most common mental disorders, affecting one in every 50 people of all ages, including children (see chapter 6), equally men and women.

To some degree, OCD-like symptoms are experienced by many healthy people, particularly in times of stress. Most of us probably 'touch wood' to avert a real or imagined danger. We check doors and windows several times before going on holiday. However, these little spells of doubts, checking or 'magical thinking' pass, while for OCD sufferers obsessive thoughts and accompanying compulsions form a never-ending cycle, which in the worst case scenario can completely take over their lives.

The best indicator of the severity of OCD is the impact on the sufferer's personal, professional and social life. The World Health Organisation lists OCD as the tenth most disabling illness, due to the loss of earning potential and diminished quality of life.

'OCD is often called "the secretive illness", as the feelings of embarrassment, guilt and shame related to the illness may prevent people from seeking help.'

Obsessions

Obsessions are intrusive images, ideas or thoughts, which keep coming into the person's mind, despite efforts to resist them. Although these thoughts are the person's own, they are disturbing, unpleasant and cause a lot of anxiety.

Obsessions can be grouped by theme:

- Dirt and contamination.
- Hoarding, saving and collecting.
- Ordering.
- Religion and morality.
- Aggressive thoughts.
- Sexual thoughts.
- Other. (For example, worry about making mistakes, the urge to remember licence plate numbers etc.)

Compulsions

Compulsions are repetitive acts or behaviours which the person feels forced to carry out, even if they know it's irrational. Attempts to resist these urges cause anxiety. Compulsions are performed in response to obsessive thoughts in order to prevent worry or lessen anxiety. However, the relief they bring is only temporary. Compulsive rituals are often accompanied by doubts that the behaviours have not been executed properly, which leads to further repetitions. This can take hours to complete and may restrict the sufferer's life to a significant degree.

Mental rituals, like repeating words, counting or saying a prayer are also compulsions, although not observable.

Compulsions can be grouped by theme too:

- Cleaning and washing.
- Checking.

- Hoarding, saving and collecting.

- Repeating, counting, ordering.

- Other. (For example, the need to confess wrong behaviour, need to touch certain items etc.)

How OCD develops

OCD can begin at any time in the person's life. Usually it starts in late teens or early twenties.

Stressful events

OCD often begins with a stressful event - food poisoning, a burglary or a fire, for example. The immediate reflection is usually that of trying to avoid a similar event in the future - by washing your hands better, checking if you've locked the door or making sure all the appliances are switched off before you leave the house. These actions seem logical, at least initially. However, there may be a moment when you realise that the fear of the event happening again hasn't diminished despite the increase in 'preventive behaviours'. The situation can then get out of control and develop into OCD.

Case Study

Richard: 'It started with food poisoning. I was very sick for a few days, and when I got better I was convinced it had happened because I hadn't washed my hands properly before cooking the dinner. I became obsessed with washing my hands and sterilising kitchen utensils before preparing any food. The rituals were taking more and more time and causing me a lot of stress. My hands were constantly sore and cracked and I had to bandage them to work. But I couldn't do my job properly with bandaged hands.

'It was my boss, whose wife had suffered similar problems, who suggested I might have OCD and should see my doctor for advice. I spoke to my GP and this was the turning point in my battle against OCD.'

Note: no specific experience has been shown to be particularly important in precipitating OCD.

Social learning

Some people may develop OCD as a consequence of 'social learning' from their parents or other significant people, who may have had OCD themselves or may have been anxious or perfectionists.

Patterns of illness

OCD can take many forms, but in general sufferers experience intrusive thoughts, impulses, images or doubts (obsessions), which keep coming back despite the efforts to fight or ignore them.

Obsessions cause a lot of anxiety, which grows as the person tries to resist the thoughts. To reduce the anxiety or neutralise the thought, the person carries out a compulsive act, which usually immediately lessens the distress associated with the thought. However, in the long run, compulsions 'feed into' obsessions and prolong the suffering.

Certain compulsions follow logically certain obsessions (e.g. hand washing as the result of fear of contamination), but sometimes there is no connection between the thought and the neutralising behaviour (e.g. an intrusive thought that something bad may happen and the compulsion to avoid cracks in the pavement to avert the danger).

Pure O

Some people may have Purely Obsessional OCD ('Pure O'), which means that they experience obsessive thoughts, but their compulsive behaviours are not visible. It is because the anxiety-reducing act is performed in the sufferer's mind, e.g. an intrusive image of running in front of a car is 'neutralised' by counting to a preferred number, or saying a mantra/prayer

Recognising the symptoms

You are likely to suffer from OCD if you have one or more symptoms from the list below.

- You worry excessively about germs and contamination. You may avoid touching dirty objects, animals, household cleaning products, shaking hands with other people.

- You can't throw anything away, even if it's useless and worn out. You collect useless objects because you think you may need them one day.

- Symmetry and order are very important to you. You spend a lot of time aligning objects like papers, books, tins, etc. in a certain, perfect, way.

- You get blasphemous or 'immoral' thoughts.

- You have irrational fears or aggressive images of harming yourself or others.

- You have unwanted and intrusive thoughts, impulses or images of a sexual nature.

- You feel an urge to remember certain things, like car number plates or slogans.

- You worry about losing things, making mistakes, saying something wrong or not right.

- You feel excessive, illogical urges to wash your hands, shower or bathe; or you may need to do it in a specific, ritualistic way.

- You have uncontrollable urges to clean, often using special cleansers or techniques, and perform it in a specific way.

- You have to avoid certain objects or places you believe to be contaminated. You wear gloves or other protection to avoid contamination.

- You have to check over and over if you've locked doors, windows, switched off appliances, etc.

- You have to check repeatedly that you did not harm yourself or others, made a mistake, or did something that may potentially cause harm.

- You need to do certain activities, like daily routines, a particular number of times.

- You feel uncontrollable urges to count bricks in walls, cars going by, windows on buildings, etc.

- You need to touch, rub, tap certain items or people.

- You feel you have to take special precautions or avoid certain objects, like knives, to prevent harm or danger.

- You feel urges to confess wrong behaviour, even if it's minor and insignificant to others.

This list is not exhaustive and is intended only to help you understand possible problem areas. OCD is best diagnosed by a doctor, so, if you think you may suffer from obsessions and/or compulsions, speak to your GP or another health care provider.

What OCD is not

The words 'obsessive' or 'compulsive' are sometimes used to describe thoughts or behaviours that don't belong to OCD. Symptoms similar to OCD can occur in the course of other mental disorders. Many repetitive behaviours may be mistakenly labelled as OCD.

OCD is not:

- Being 'obsessive' about shoes, football, a hobby, etc, or a being a 'compulsive liar'. Although these people spend a lot of time thinking and/or doing one thing over and over again, it isn't usually a problem to them. Moreover, they enjoy these activities, while OCD behaviours are never pleasurable.

- Compulsive gambling and other addictions, like drugs or alcohol. These behaviours may be seen as compulsive because of the urge the person feels, but obsessive thoughts and compulsions are unwanted and never bring any pleasure, unlike the addictions.

- Superstitions, repetitive behaviours and rituals arising from cultural or religious beliefs. Many people are superstitious. Rituals and repetitive behaviours are part of everyday lives in many cultures (funeral rituals, initiation rites in certain societies or fraternities, prayers used to overcome bad thoughts or concentrate on a task). Usually, these thoughts or behaviours are neither intrusive, nor compulsory; there is no resistance, they make perfect sense in the cultural context and never take over the person's life.

- Eating disorders. 'Obsessive' preoccupation with food, thinness and calorie counting, anorexia, bulimia, or 'compulsive overeating' (binge eating) may resemble OCD, but these are eating disorders. However, it is important to remember that OCD often accompanies anorexia.

- Psychosis, particularly schizophrenia. Intrusive thoughts or rituals similar to OCD may also be present in psychosis or schizophrenia. Unlike in OCD, the sufferer perceives these thoughts or actions as not their own, but as if they were inserted into his/her mind or imposed by someone else.

- Body dysmorphic disorder (BDD). Obsession with ugliness (see chapter 7 for more details).

'The words "obsessive" or "compulsive" are sometimes used to describe thoughts or behaviours that don't belong to OCD. Symptoms similar to OCD can occur in course of other mental disorders. Many repetitive behaviours may be mistakenly labelled as OCD.'

■ Autism Spectrum Disorders. Children with some forms of autism, like Aspergers' syndrome, need order and routines because it helps them to feel less anxious.

Illness or personality?

Obsessive-compulsive personality disorder (American term) or anankastic personality disorder (term used in the UK and Europe) is different from OCD. Although OCPD shares some features with OCD, these are two separate disorders. People with OCPD are preoccupied with detail, rules, lists and, generally speaking, order. They are well-organised perfectionists with great attention to detail. They are usually cautious, prefer routine, predictability and repetition, and struggle with anything which is not black-or-white. These traits develop through adolescence and early adulthood, and as part of their personality, feel 'in harmony' with the person, even if their family, friends or work colleagues see them as problematic.

For people who suffer from OCD, urges for perfectionism, cleanliness and order are perceived as uncomfortable and problematic. They know they would be happier without these symptoms.

Summing Up

Obessive-compulsive disorder (OCD) is an anxiety-related condition, which affects one in every 50 people at any stage in life, regardless of their gender, class or ethnicity. Intrusive, unwanted thoughts and images or doubts are sources of extreme anxiety. Compulsive acts are carried out with the intention to neutralise these feelings but they are time-consuming and bring only temporary relief from obsessions, reinforcing the vicious cycle in the long run.

'Obessive-compulsive disorder (OCD) is an anxiety-related condition, which affects one in every 50 people at any stage in life, regardless of their gender, class or ethnicity.'

Chapter Two

What Causes OCD?

Unfortunately, it is still not clear what exactly causes OCD. It is a disorder with many faces, and sometimes one person can have different sets of symptoms at different periods of time (e.g. tidying and lining up items as a young adult, hand washing and fear of contamination later in life). There are several factors that can potentially lead to developing OCD and every sufferer may have a different combination of them. This makes the search for the causes of the illness even more difficult.

Biological factors

As medication (see chapter 3 for more details) is an effective treatment for OCD, it is natural to assume that there may be some biological background to the disorder. Indeed, brain imaging studies show that people with OCD have different blood flow patterns in certain parts of their brain compared to those without the disorder. Interestingly, these patterns change and resemble healthy ones with effective treatment, whether it is medication or CBT (cognitive behavioural therapy).

Although scientists still have not found the exact mechanism in which OCD develops, the theory that it is the result of a chemical imbalance of serotonin in the brain is widely accepted.

'OCD is a disorder with many faces, and sometimes one person can have different sets of symptoms at different periods of time.'

OCD and infections

In some children OCD develops after a streptococcal infection (Streptococcus is a bacteria causing a common throat infection). Antibodies produced by our immune system as the natural defence mechanism, react with parts of our brain, which is believed to be the trigger for PANDAS - Paediatric Autoimmune Neuropsychiatric Disorders Associated with streptococcus (see chapter 6 for more details).

Does OCD run in families?

'Although the mechanism is not entirely clear, a person with OCD is four times more likely to have another family member struggling with the illness than the general population.'

There have been a number of studies which looked into the possibility of OCD being inherited in genes. Although the mechanism is not entirely clear, a person with OCD is four times more likely, than the general population, to have another family member struggling with the illness.

The family of tics?

Studies show that OCD sufferers are more likely to have relatives with tics or Tourette's syndrome, but the exact mechanism is not clear.

Some specialists believe that OCD is related to other disorders characterised by urges to carry out certain unwanted behaviours, like tics or Tourette's syndrome (see chapter 7 for more details). It has even been suggested that OCD behaviours can be seen as 'tics of the mind'.

Can OCD be learnt from your parents?

Another theory is that OCD is 'inherited' by children from their parents not genetically, but as a learnt behaviour. However, there is no evidence to prove this link. The same goes for speculation that overprotective parents are more likely to bring up children struggling with OCD; or findings that some childhood experiences are common to OCD sufferers. On the other hand, stress and tensions within the family, and particularly if provoked by the OCD symptoms, may contribute to the onset or an exacerbation of OCD.

Which aspect of OCD may be family-related?

Finding the link between OCD and the family is difficult because there are so many different factors at play and it is hard to separate one from the other. Some family related factors include:

- Biological predispositions, which may be related to your genes, environment in the womb and after the birth.
- Psychological experiences of the members of your particular family.
- Sociocultural background of your family.
- At some stage, the family involvement in rituals and requests for reassurance become almost an integral part of the illness, or even a maintaining factor.

Psychological factors

There have been several studies done to help understand the psychological factors involved in OCD.

The role of live events

'Life events and increased stress levels can worsen existing OCD symptoms.'

One line of research tried to see if there were any particular life events that were more likely to trigger OCD. There is evidence that childhood trauma and abuse are linked with the subsequent development of depression and anxiety disorders, including phobias and OCD. However, the connections are unclear and it is probably more important how the event is perceived and interpreted by the person rather that the event itself. Even positive events have the potential to trigger OCD.

Life events and increased stress levels can worsen existing OCD symptoms.

Sometimes the theme of the life event preceding the onset or worsening (a flare-up) of OCD is reflected in the symptoms (e.g. in Richard's case, as described in chapter 1, when food poisoning triggered off excessive worries about contamination and subsequent hand washing), but this may not mean that this particular event is the cause of the illness.

Generally speaking, life events are more likely to be triggers if the person experiencing them already has a biological or psychological predisposition to OCD.

Interpretations and beliefs

The current psychological understanding of how OCD develops emphasises the role of the way people interpret their thoughts and what beliefs they hold. There is some evidence that OCD sufferers are more likely to have perfectionistic beliefs, think that they are responsible for harm to others and that they need to control their thoughts.

What keeps it going?

Unfortunately, in the majority of cases, it is impossible to identify the exact cause of OCD. Very often, it's a combination of factors which have come together at the same time. To understand and successfully treat OCD, it is important to identify these key elements:

- Predisposing factors (e.g. biological, psychological, family-related).
- Precipitating factors (triggers, like life events; stress; physical illness).
- Maintaining factors (what keeps it going).

Predisposing and precipitating factors have been discussed above, and hopefully you are now able to better understand these elements of the illness.

You have no influence over your genetic predisposition, or other biological vulnerabilities. You cannot turn back the time and avoid psychological experiences that contributed to your OCD. You can, however, look at the mechanisms that keep the vicious cycle of obsessions and compulsions going and try to break it.

The paradox of mental suppression

Understanding how obsessive thoughts work is one of the most important things in trying to overcome them. Paradoxically, trying not to think about a particular thing will only keep the thought coming back to your mind. This was proven in a study developed by professor D. Wegner and his colleagues (Wegner at al., 1987), who asked the participants not to think about a white bear. The results revealed that the more people try to suppress a certain thought, the more they are likely to think about it. The same goes for unwanted thoughts and images – attempts at pushing them out of your mind will result in the obsessions returning to your mind.

The futility of the rituals

If you are unsure whether or not you've locked the door when you left home this morning, a simple solution seems to be to go back and check. If you can't leave the office or have gone away on holiday, you may ask a family member, a friend or a trusted neighbour to pop round and check it for you. If you worry that your hands may have become contaminated by germs because you've touched a dirty surface, the natural way of dealing with that would be to wash your hands, or even disinfect them.

Checking and reassurance work in normal circumstances, but when OCD comes into play, the dynamics change. You have probably already realised that checking, asking for reassurance or performing a ritual will bring you only temporary relief from your anxiety. In fact, this behaviour is likely to reinforce your belief that carrying out the compulsion prevents bad things from happening. So next time, you feel even more pressure to go back to the house and check the door again, and again, and again.

Vicious cycle

A similar mechanism strengthens the vicious cycle of 'neutralising behaviours' - acts or thoughts that are applied to counteract your obsessions, like saying a prayer, repeating a certain phrase, or touching wood to avert a danger. These types of symptoms often occur in so-called 'pure obsessions' (Pure O), where disturbing thoughts are accompanied by mental compulsions. Mental compulsions happen in the sufferer's mind, so they are not visible. However, these attempts at neutralising the initial obsessive thoughts are also ineffective at fighting the illness, and they are likely to reinforce it.

The role of family and friends

Family and friends are great sources of support and often practical help for OCD sufferers. When you see your loved one overwhelmed with worry or anxiety, it is only natural to try to help. Unfortunately, responding to requests for reassurance can alleviate the distress of OCD only in the short term. In the longer run, these attempts are unhelpful and can actually contribute in maintaining OCD.

Case Study

Pam: 'I had constant worries that something bad might happen to my family, so I developed a system to check if they were OK. My husband and children had to 'check-in' every so often, either by calling me or sending me a text message. If any of them were late with their 'check-in' my anxiety would heighten and I would keep calling them until I could get hold of them.

'Soon, it wasn't enough, so I started asking other family members, friends, teachers, work colleagues, anyone I could think of to check on them on my behalf. It spread like wildfire until my family were exhausted and exasperated by my constant requests, and my husband took me to see my doctor.'

For advice on how to break the cycle of unhelpful involvement in maintaining OCD, see chapter 5.

Understanding your OCD

As mentioned previously, successful treatment of your OCD depends on your understanding of possible causes, as well as identifying maintaining factors. Understanding of the illness starts with a very simple step of recognising your problems as symptoms of an illness – obsessive-compulsive disorder.

It's not your fault

Having read this chapter, you know that although the exact cause is not known, there is enough evidence to suspect that OCD is somewhat the result of a chemical imbalance in your brain, which is something you don't have control over. Remember - OCD is not yours or anybody else's fault. Gaining this understanding may help you overcome the embarrassment and shame, which often prevents OCD sufferers from seeking help.

Masters of our minds?

We, as human beings, strive to be in control of our bodies and minds. The belief that we are able to master our thoughts and actions is tricky in OCD. As you have seen, attempts at controlling your unwanted thoughts by suppressing ('neutralising') them, asking for reassurance, performing checks or other rituals, seem to be counter-productive in the long term.

Helpful strategies

Awareness of the futility of attempts to control your thoughts is vital in understanding how you can help yourself. Specialists advise that you should not resist your obsessive thoughts, but expose yourself to them instead. It may sound counter-intuitive, but it has been proven to work in reducing anxiety caused by obsessions.

A helpful approach to compulsive acts is different and it actually encourages the sufferer to resist his/her compulsions.

These two strategies reflect the principles of ERP (exposure and response prevention) approach to OCD and are discussed in more detail in chapter 3.

A structured approach to understanding your OCD and helping yourself recover from it is presented in 'The Four Steps' by Dr. Jeffrey Schwartz, which is available free at OCD-UK website You can access it by going to http://www.ocduk.org and then clicking on 'Four Steps Self-Help' in the site's Contents column).

Understanding the nature of your obsessions and compulsions, and the mechanism which keeps them going is often the first step on the journey to recovery. Whatever the causes, OCD is a treatable illness and help and support are available.

'Gaining the understanding that OCD is not yours or anybody else's fault, may help you overcome the embarrassment and shame, which often prevents OCD sufferers from seeking help.'

Summing Up

OCD is an illness with many faces and despite extensive research into the nature of it, the exact cause has not been found. There are several factors at play, with biological and psychological theories providing multiple explanations, however it is very difficult to pinpoint the 'culprit' in individual cases. For many sufferers, their OCD is most likely to be the result of a number of different elements coming together.

While fighting the illness, it is important to understand which behaviours are helpful and which are likely to keep the vicious cycle of OCD going. This can be a valid step in breaking free from your obsessions and compulsions.

Remember, whatever the cause of your illness, OCD is treatable and help and support are available.

Chapter Three

Treatment Explained

So, you have talked to your doctor about your problems and you now have the diagnosis of OCD. Good news – you are on the right path to taking control over your illness and getting your life back on track. Many people with OCD find this first step very, if not the most, difficult. Hopefully you feel relieved that there is a name to your problem and ways of resolving it. But on the other hand, you may worry about different aspects of living with a mental illness, which treatment you should choose, how long it's going to take for you to get better and how you can make it happen.

Making informed decisions about your treatment

Once you have a diagnosis, you can start making informed decisions about your treatment. Take time to think about it. Don't be afraid to ask your doctor as many questions as you need. You may also seek further help by speaking to a therapist, a trusted friend or family member, or any of the organisations that support people with OCD (see the Help List at the end of the book). This is the beginning of an arduous journey, but with the promise of fantastic reward – relief from your obsessive-compulsive symptoms.

'A journey of a thousand miles begins with a single step.'

Confucius.

OCD is a well-known illness and a range of therapeutic interventions have been developed. The discoveries of new antidepressant drugs and CBT over the last 30 years have transformed the treatment of OCD, bringing new hope to the sufferers and their families.

Medication

Medication has proved to be an effective treatment for OCD, however its action usually develops gradually over time. You may need to wait weeks, sometimes even months, to see any improvement in your condition. Experts suggest waiting at least 12 weeks to see if the drug is effective for you or not. It may feel frustrating to wait that long, but it is important to continue taking your medication exactly as prescribed.

Antidepressants and OCD

Antidepressants and, specifically, selective serotonin reuptake inhibitors (SSRIs) have been used to treat OCD since the 1980s. These drugs increase the level of a specific brain chemical (neurotransmitter) called serotonin by suppressing its reuptake, so that there is more serotonin left to interact with brain cells. Serotonin is involved in the mechanism which underlies depression.

The mechanism in which antidepressants work in OCD is not entirely clear, but it is believed that OCD is somehow caused by a malfunctioning of the serotonin system in our brain. So don't worry that you are being prescribed an antidepressant even if you are not depressed. Some antidepressants are recommended in OCD.

Medication recommended for OCD

Not all antidepressants have been found to be beneficial in OCD, but only those which are powerful inhibitors of serotonin reuptake (serotonin reuptake inhibitors – SRIs). Among several classes of antidepressants currently available on the market, only SSRIs and one particular drug from another group called tricyclics are recommended as effective.

The antidepressants recommended by National Institute for Health and Clinical Excellence (NICE) for OCD are:

- Citalopram (Celexa, Cipramil).
- Fluoxetine (Prozac, Seronil, Fontex).
- Fluvoxamine (Faverin).
- Paroxetine (Paroxil, Paxil, Senoxet).
- Sertraline (Zoloft, Lustral).
- Clomipramine (Anafranil).

The first name is the generic name (non-proprietary title) of the drug. Names in the brackets are brand names (proprietary titles), which are only given for your information as examples and may differ in different countries. If you have any questions regarding prescribed medication, speak to your doctor or pharmacist.

Clomipramine

Clomipramine is a tricyclic antidepressant, the first one to be discovered as beneficial in OCD. Due to potential side effects, clomipramine is currently considered as a 'second line' treatment, which means that it should not be prescribed to those who have never been prescribed any of the above listed SSRIs.

Effectiveness of the medication

All of the listed drugs have been found to be equally effective, however SSRIs may be better tolerated. It is impossible to determine which of these drugs will be effective for you without trying them, unless you have taken one of these drugs in the past. The choice of the medication is a decision made by you and your doctor (see chapter 4 for advice on how you can get involved in this process).

Generally speaking, antidepressants are effective for six out of 10 OCD sufferers who have been prescribed them.

Addictive?

You may need to take your medication for a long time and so it is important that you remember SSRIs and clomipramine are not addictive. Sometimes, if you forget to take your tablets as prescribed, you may experience unpleasant symptoms, like trembling, sweating, confusion, nausea or insomnia. These are withdrawal (discontinuation) symptoms and are caused by the way these drugs work, and not by physical dependence on them. If you experience any of these symptoms or want to know more about them, talk to your doctor.

Anxiolytics

Anxiolytics are drugs that ease anxiety. The most popular anxiolytics are benzodiazepines, e.g. diazepam, clonazepam, lorazepam. Although these drugs may bring some relief from OCD, they should not be prescribed routinely because of the risk of dependency they are known to cause.

Antipsychotics

Antipsychotics are drugs used for the treatment of different types of psychosis - a mental disorder where people develop unusual beliefs or can see or hear things that are not there. Antipsychotics can sometimes be prescribed in OCD, but it does not mean that you have a psychotic illness. These drugs can be helpful in certain situations. If your symptoms are particularly severe or not responding well to the previous treatment, your doctor may suggest adding an antipsychotic to your current medication.

General information on taking medication

If you are taking any medication for your OCD it is important that you:

- Discuss possible side effects with your doctor and ask for advice on what to do if any of these occur.

- Inform your doctor of any other medication, herbal remedies or supplements you are taking, or any drug allergies and special dietary requirements you have. It is important that your doctor knows of these before prescribing your medication as they may change the effect of your medication, or your medication may affect the way the other agents work.

- Tell your doctor if you are pregnant, or intending to become pregnant, are breastfeeding or wish to breastfeed.

- If you feel unwell or suspect an adverse reaction to the drug you are taking, contact your doctor, or seek medical attention immediately.

- Read the medication leaflet carefully and seek medical help if you develop any of the listed side effects.

- Take the medication exactly as prescribed. Don't change the dosage and don't stop taking it altogether without talking to your doctor first.

- Be careful when driving or operating any machinery until you know how your medication affects you.

- Try to avoid drinking alcohol while talking your OCD medication. These drugs don't mix well with alcohol and can even be a dangerous combination. Also, the long-term effect of alcohol on your OCD may be detrimental (see chapter 8 for more details on how you can help yourself to get better and stay well).

Psychological interventions

Psychological interventions (therapies) have been used in OCD for a long time and over the years experts have gathered evidence on the effectiveness of different therapeutic approaches.

Cognitive behavioural therapy (CBT)

CBT has been used successfully in the treatment of OCD since the 1970s. This approach provides you with tools to challenge your obsessive thoughts and compulsions. It may seem hard and even scary at times, particularly at the beginning of your journey, but it has been proven to be successful for 75% of those who try it.

Exposure and response prevention (ERP)

ERP is a form of cognitive behavioural therapy, employing the process of habituation, in which our nervous system gets used to a stimulus through repeated, prolonged contact. The idea is to reduce anxiety and discomfort associated with the symptoms by exposing yourself to your obsessions. Exposure to obsessions happens in small steps and provides 'emotional numbness' to the situation, which originally provoked anxiety. The ultimate goal is complete habituation to the feared situation or object.

The response prevention part of ERP focuses on decreasing the frequency of rituals by resisting the urge to perform the ritual. This process is usually gradual, moving from delaying the performance of the ritual by longer periods, towards the ultimate goal of being able to block the ritual completely.

CBT and ERP – practicalities

CBT and ERP can be delivered individually through structured self-help materials, over the phone, in person; or in a group situation.

'Exposure to obsessions happens is small steps and provides 'emotional numbness' to the situation, which originally provoked anxiety. The ultimate goal is complete habituation to the feared situation or object.'

The length of treatment depends on the severity of the symptoms. NICE suggests up to 10 therapist hours for mild OCD, and longer therapy in more complex cases.

Cognitive Therapy (CT)

Cognitive therapy focuses on your obsessional thoughts and aims at changing the ways you respond to them. It targets self-critical beliefs and intrusive thoughts by provoking you to weigh up evidence for and against your ideas. It also helps you to relax and resist your obsessions.

Cognitive therapy has been found helpful in cases of 'pure obsessions', where the rituals are performed in the sufferer's mind, and are not visible.

CT may be added to ERP in an attempt to enhance its effectiveness.

Psychoanalysis

Psychoanalysis is a long-term, intensive psychotherapeutic approach developed in late 19th, early 20th century by Sigmund Freud. It is based on exploration of the person's unconscious thought processes to find the causes for certain symptoms and areas of resistance, which are believed to block emotional growth and prevent changes. Psychoanalysis is still used, although in slightly different ways and it is not as popular as it has been in the past.

In the 1960s, other, more effective therapeutic tools, like CBT, ERP and medication were developed and are now more widely used. Psychoanalysis may still be available as an option in some parts of England and Wales, however NICE (National Institute for Health and Clinical Excellence) guidance for OCD suggests that there is not enough evidence of efficacy or effectiveness of psychoanalysis in OCD.

Other psychological interventions

Although CBT has proved very effective in the treatment of OCD, there are limits to its utility. Not every OCD sufferer will benefit from this approach; and a proportion of those who start therapy do not complete it for various reasons, e.g. because they find ERP too difficult. It is therefore useful to know if there are other psychological interventions that could be beneficial.

Meditation

Meditation has been suggested to be helpful in reducing symptoms of OCD, however, to date, there is not enough evidence to support this claim.

Couple or family therapy

These interventions focus on problems in a relationship/family, and although not recommended for OCD, may be helpful if you have other problems beside OCD. It may also help your family/partner understand OCD and how they can help you get better.

Hypnosis

Some people have found hypnosis beneficial in reducing their obsessive-compulsive symptoms, however there is not enough evidence to recommend hypnosis or hypnotherapy as a specific OCD treatment.

Counselling

Many people find talking about their thoughts and feelings beneficial, however the evidence shows that in OCD facing our fears works better than talking about them.

Combined and intensive interventions

ERP and medication are generally effective in reducing obsessions and compulsions, but none of these interventions work 100% for everyone. Some people are unable to tolerate the side effects of the medication or anxiety experienced during ERP. Sometimes, the relief from OCD is only limited whatever the treatment method used. In those situations your doctor may suggest a combined or intensive intervention. This usually requires a referral to specialist mental health teams with access to psychiatrists, psychologists, psychiatric nurses, CBT therapists, etc.

Medication plus CBT (including ERP)

The most common combined intervention is the mixture of medication and CBT (including ERP). NICE recommends that this combination should be offered to people with moderate and severe OCD, as there is evidence that it works better than ERP or medication alone.

'CBT (including ERP) helps 75% of sufferers while medication helps around 60%.'

Adding an antipsychotic

If your symptoms are particularly severe or not responding well to the previous treatment, your doctor may suggest adding an antipsychotic drug, such as risperidone, olanzapine or quetiapine, to the medication already prescribed.

Two anti-OCD drugs

Taking two anti-OCD drugs at the same time (e.g. citalopram and clomipramine) is another way of enhancing the effects of your medication.

Hospital admission

The majority of OCD sufferers will improve with the treatment provided by their GP, a specialist outpatient clinic or community team. However, a small proportion of patients with very severe symptoms, particularly if they are unable to attend the clinic because of their OCD, may need an admission to hospital for intensive treatment. You may also be offered this option if you suffer from additional mental health problems, suicidal thoughts, or you are unable to look after yourself properly.

Other help

Support groups

It helps to feel that you are not alone in your struggle against your illness. Being part of an OCD support group can give you an opportunity to come together with other sufferers, share coping strategies, encourage one another, and just make friends.

To find your local group ask at your clinic, GP surgery or your local newspaper. You can also find details at www.ocduk.org and click on 'support groups'.

Guided self-help

There are several self-help guide books, tapes, videos and software programs devised specifically for OCD. You can find some recommendations on the websites listed below:

www.ocduk.org - click on 'Treatments', then 'Self-Help'.

www.anxietyuk.org.uk - click on 'Shop', then 'Obsessive-Compulsive Disorder'.

www.rcpsych.ac.uk - click on 'Mental Health Info', then choose 'Obessive-Compulsive Disorder' from the list and scroll down for 'further reading' recommendations.

There are more suggestions in the Help List at the back of this book.

Computerised therapies

CBT has been adapted to be used on the computer (standalone PC or via the Internet) and studies show that this method is also successful in helping people with depression or anxiety disorders.

The program developed to address specific OCD problems (OCFighter, previously known as BTSteps) is not currently recommended by NICE (as per NICE OCD guidance updated September 2008) and is only available to those who have been in the program for a while or through research.

Complementary and alternative therapies

Although some people may find acupuncture, herbal remedies or homoeopathy beneficial to their general wellbeing, there is no medical evidence that any of them work in OCD.

Summing Up

You have just made the first step on your journey to recovery – you've talked to your doctor about your problems and you've got the diagnosis of obessive-compulsive disorder. Now you are going to grab the opportunity to break free from your OCD and get your life back on track. You have a choice of cognitive and behavioural therapies and antidepressants to help you get the illness under control.

CBT is generally recommended to all sufferers, but those with severe symptoms, limited improvement, severe anxiety or those who otherwise would have to wait a long time for therapy, may be offered antidepressant medication.

It is important that you follow your treatment as prescribed and inform your doctor of any side effects. If you have any doubts about your treatment, talk to your doctor or therapist.

Chapter Four

Getting Help

You suspect you may have OCD and you have decided to seek help. What is the next step? Where should you start your journey to recovery?

When, how and where to seek help

The first step

As with any illness, whether it involves your body or mind, your own family doctor is always the best person to talk to in the first place. GPs, by definition, have good knowledge of common health problems, understanding of local community and healthcare services, they also know their patients well. Your doctor will be able to confirm (or not) your diagnosis and suggest the best way forward.

Seeking help – when?

Many OCD sufferers find disclosing their symptoms, even to family, friends or healthcare professionals, very difficult. They often feel guilty, embarrassed or ashamed by their symptoms, particularly if they experience intrusive thoughts of a violent nature. Some people fear the stigma and the consequences of being diagnosed with a mental illness. Unfortunately, these difficulties frequently result in postponing the first visit to the doctor and seeking help. Sometimes there is a long gap of several years between the onset of the symptoms and the correct diagnosis and treatment.

When should you seek help then? As soon as you realise you may have OCD. The sooner you do it, the sooner you can access treatment and find relief from your symptoms.

Can it go away?

In mild cases of OCD, symptoms may improve without any intervention. Some people may experience bouts of obsessive thoughts or compulsions at certain times of their lives (often stress-related) and remain symptom-free in-between. However, if your symptoms are more severe, even if they wax and wane, they are less likely to disappear, and may get worse with time.

Where should you go?

Booking an appointment with your GP is a good place to start your journey towards recovery. GPs are becoming more and more aware of OCD, but it is always good to go to your appointment well prepared (see below for some pointers).

What will my doctor do?

NICE guidelines for OCD suggest that if your OCD symptoms are mild, which means that they impact on your life or functioning only slightly, your doctor may decide to start the treatment within primary care. You may be advised to try structured, self-help CBT (including ERP) first, or attend a series of up to 10 sessions in a group, individually, or over the phone.

Will I be prescribed any medication?

If you need medication this will be prescribed and monitored by your GP.

If your OCD does not respond to initial treatment, or if your life is significantly affected by the symptoms, your GP may refer you to a specialised primary care team or secondary services. If this is your case, your treatment will be delivered and supervised by a specialist team, consisting of psychiatric nurses, CBT therapists, psychologists and psychiatrists.

'In mild cases of OCD, symptoms may improve without any intervention. Some people may experience bouts of obsessive thoughts or compulsions at certain times of their lives (often stress-related) and remain symptom-free in-between.'

Sometimes, particularly for people with severe symptoms, or other co-existing mental health problems (particularly suicidal thoughts), a hospital admission or referral to an intensive treatment programme may be considered.

How to seek help

Booking an appointment with your GP may be the easiest part of seeking help. Many people with mental health problems struggle to talk about their difficulties because of embarrassment, difficulty in expressing their psychological distress, or for the fear of being misunderstood. Disclosing the symptoms may be even harder for OCD sufferers due to the nature of their thoughts (see above). If you are concerned that you may find talking to your GP difficult, ask a trusted family member or a friend to assist you during the appointment. You may also write your symptoms and questions down on a piece of paper, take it with you and just read it out if need be. If you feel you may need more time than the usual 10-minute appointment, request a double appointment.

GP ice breaker

OCD-UK, the leading UK charity working for people with OCD, developed a special 'GP ice breaker' – a brief message to your GP/health care professional you can simply print off from their website (www.ocduk.org then go to 'Treatments' and click on 'GP Ice Breaker'). You can amend it if you want by adding or crossing off symptoms. Hand the completed document in to your doctor during the appointment.

Be open and honest

It is important that you are as open and honest about your symptoms as possible. If you are feeling depressed, have thoughts of harming yourself or others, or any other psychological symptoms that worry you, tell your doctor about them as well. The better your doctor can understand your problem, the more likely he/she is to diagnose it and suggest the most suitable treatment for you.

Choosing the right health professional

It is impossible to determine which health professional will be right for you without first knowing how severe your symptoms are. Your preferences should also be taken into consideration when your options are discussed. Unfortunately, your choice may be limited by the availability of certain treatments in your area, or waiting lists.

Ultimately, the right health professional is the one you can trust and work together with. Don't hesitate to express your opinion on the options offered to you, particularly if you have any reservations about working with this particular health professional.

'It is important that you are as open and honest about your symptoms as possible. The better your doctor can understand your problem, the more likely he/she is to diagnose it and suggest the most suitable treatment for you.'

Medication or therapy?

Making decisions about your treatment is not easy, but your doctor will be able to help you. Make sure you have all the information you need. Don't be afraid to ask questions if there is anything you don't understand. If you find it difficult to speak, or remember what you wanted to ask – make a list of questions or ask a family member or a friend to accompany you to your appointment.

Which treatment is most effective?

Both medication and CBT therapies have been found to be effective for OCD. ERP is slightly more effective than antidepressants, as it helps around 75% of people who try it, however it may not be suitable for everyone. Unfortunately, some people who start the therapy are unable to complete it, and among those who succeed, a quarter may have a relapse of the illness at some point in the future and require extra treatment.

Medication helps around 60% of OCD sufferers. It works by reducing the intensity of the symptoms ('taking the edge off'), which remain under control as long as the medication is taken. Although, half of the people who stop taking the tablets will get the symptoms again, unless they receive the therapy as well.

Which approach is suitable for me?

Every case is individual and there is no 'one size fits all' solution. It is therefore important that you talk openly and honestly about not only your symptoms but also your fears and expectations. Unfortunately, sometimes external factors, like waiting lists or funding issues, may limit available options, but you should always be offered legitimate, effective treatment.

Please refer to the NICE guidelines for further information (go to www.nice. org.uk, click on 'Find Guidance', then 'NICE Guidance by Topic', then 'Mental Health and Behavioural Conditions' and scroll down the list to find obsessive-compulsive disorder), or see chapter 3 for details on available treatments.

Who is the therapy best for?

NICE guidelines suggests that CBT therapy, including ERP, should be recommended in any case of OCD, irrespective of the severity. If your symptoms affect your life only in a mild degree, e.g. you are still able to lead a fairly normal life, you will be offered low intensity psychological treatments, including ERP. It may be suggested that you try structured self-help materials, are referred for group CBT, or try short individual therapy over the phone. This approach usually involves up to 10 hours of therapeutic sessions.

Are there any side effects with therapy?

Although therapy also helps re-establish the biochemical balance in your brain, it is not a chemical substance, so it does not produce side effects the way medication does. However, as ERP involves being exposed to the unpleasant and distressing obsessions, some people find it too difficult to engage in the therapy.

Who is the medication best for?

As suggested by the NICE guidelines, medication should be offered to people with moderate and severe OCD, as well as to those who have found therapy unsuccessful or who are unable to engage in CBT. The medication should be offered as a choice, or in combination with CBT (if the symptoms are severe).

Not recommended?

There are a number of situations when medication is contraindicated or should be prescribed with caution. If this is the case with you, your doctor will talk it through with you. If you have ever been prescribed any of the anti-OCD medication and had a bad reaction to it, tell your doctor about it.

'NICE guidelines suggests that CBT therapy, including ERP, should be recommended in any case of OCD, irrespective of the severity.'

Questions you may want to ask your doctor

Before you make your choice of treatment, it is important that you understand what it entails and how it may affect you. Your doctor will be able to provide you with necessary information or point you to another reliable source. If you have any questions, don't hesitate to ask.

It is useful to write your questions down before you see your doctor, so you don't forget about something important.

Here is a list of common questions:

- How does the medication/therapy work to help my OCD symptoms?
- How long before I will see any improvement?
- Are there any side effects?
- What should I do if side effects occur?
- How should I take my medication?
- How long should I take the medication/go for therapy?
- What if the treatment does not work?

Choosing the right therapy/therapist

The right therapy

As per NICE guidelines for OCD recommendations, you should be offered cognitive behavioural treatments, including the exposure and response prevention approach (ERP). If you are unable to engage in ERP, you may be offered individual cognitive therapy.

No other type of therapy has been found to be as beneficial in OCD as CBT, (see chapter 3 for more information), therefore you should be offered CBT whether on the NHS, or privately. If you have other problems you want to address, like relationship difficulties, talk to your health care professional about it - they should be able to advise you on the best way forward.

Finding the therapist

If you receive treatment funded by public services (e.g. through your GP's surgery) you are likely to be referred to a therapist or a therapy centre contracted by your health care provider. In this case, your choice of therapist may be limited.

If you decide to seek help in the private sector you may still ask your GP for recommendations. You may want to use the local Yellow Pages, or ask family or friends for recommendations. Professional organisations for psychotherapists usually have registers accessible to the general public. You can browse their registers searching for a qualified therapist specialising in OCD in a chosen geographical area. See the help list section of this book for instructions.

Qualifications

There are a number of ways people can train to be CBT therapists. The training usually involves a course or several courses of different lengths, depending on the type of studies and intended outcome; as well as a certain amount of practical experience (conducting the actual therapy under supervision).

In the UK, it usually takes 1-2 years to become a fully qualified CBT therapist. However, often mental health professionals, like CPNs (community psychiatric nurses) or OTs (occupational therapists) do shorter courses to learn CBT skills essential in their work with their patients. These professionals usually have other therapeutic skills and use supervision provided by CBT specialists, to ensure that the therapy they deliver is appropriate.

Recommendations?

OCD-UK recommend using a therapist accredited by the British Association for Behavioural Cognitive Psychotherapies (BABCP), the lead organisation for CBT in the UK.

To become an accredited member of BABCP, the therapist has to meet and maintain certain criteria (see www.babcp.com for details). BABCP have a database of their members, and you can search it by going to www.babcp.com, clicking on the 'Find a therapist' section, choosing 'Obessive-compulsive disorders' from the drop-down menu, and entering your local area details.

Whether you are referred to an NHS therapist or go private, don't be afraid to ask about their qualifications, professional credentials, experience or approach. In fact, if you have any issues related to the therapist or therapy, you should talk to your therapist first.

What should I ask the therapist?

Any therapy relies strongly on the therapeutic alliance – the unique relationship of trust between the person who is in therapy (the client) and the therapist. As trust is something that we build over a period of time, at first your therapy will have to rely on the 'credit of trust'. You need to feel that you can engage in therapy with this particular person. Don't be afraid to ask as many questions as you need. Here are suggestions of what you may want to ask your therapist:

- What qualifications do you have?
- Do you receive supervision?
- How much experience in treating OCD have you got?

'Whether you are referred to an NHS therapist or go private, don't be afraid to ask about their qualifications, professional credentials, experience or approach.'

- How often will you see me?
- How long is a session?
- How many sessions will I have?
- Will I be involved in setting the goals?
- What happens if I cannot come to a session? (If you decide to go private you also need to clarify the financial implications of a cancelled session.)
- What happens if a session is cancelled by the therapist?
- Will I get any 'home work'?
- How long before I can see any effects?
- What if I need extra support between the sessions?
- What will a typical session look like?

Summing Up

'Every journey starts with the first step', so goes the saying. Your first step on your way to breaking free from OCD should be your own doctor, and you should make it as soon as possible. When talking about your problem, try to be as open and honest with your GP as you can. This will help your doctor understand the extent of your symptoms, assess any risks and advise you on the best treatment options. Whether you will be offered therapy, medication or a mix of both, don't be afraid to ask all the necessary questions. You need to feel well informed to be able to make the right choices. You are making decisions about your health, after all.

Chapter Five

Caring for Someone with OCD

A secret illness

OCD is called a secret illness, as it often goes undiagnosed for years because sufferers feel too embarrassed, guilty or ashamed to seek help. Although it is possible to hide the symptoms to some degree, it involves a lot of effort and sooner or later family or friends realise that something is not quite right.

Case Study

Margaret: 'I've always been the one who made sure that all the doors and windows were locked and kitchen appliances switched off before I went to bed. The checking got worse with the stress of moving to a new house in a not-so-good area. I thought I still had it under control because I was doing it quietly at night when everyone was asleep. One night I got so stuck in repeating my rituals, I didn't notice my husband on the landing watching me.

'Even when he confronted me, I tried to argue that I wasn't doing anything out of the ordinary. But he told me he'd started suspecting something since I'd broken a door handle. He'd been woken up by the noise of doors being opened and closed repeatedly a couple of times before, but never managed to catch me until that night. After a long, honest chat I agreed to seek help and I'm glad I did.'

Recognising OCD signs

Although everyone is different, there are certain themes along which OCD symptoms can be grouped (see chapter 1 for details). Here is a list of typical signs suggesting that your loved one may be suffering from OCD:

- Cracked, sore or even bleeding hands.
- Excessive cleaning even when the place looks clean and tidy.
- Preoccupation with order and neatness, insisting that things are organised in a certain way (e.g. alphabetically, according to the size) and getting upset if they are not.
- Spending a lot of time completing routine activities, trying to get it done 'just right'.
- Being late for work, school, appointments etc., because of checking and rechecking.
- Frequent urges to go back and 'double check' if the door is locked, oven switched off, etc.
- Unwarranted concerns about other people's safety, frequent need to check on their family or friends.
- Unreasonable reassurance seeking.
- Having rigid routines and/or rituals and becoming upset when these are disturbed.
- Accumulating useless objects, inability to throw anything away, because 'I may need it one day'.
- 'Magical thinking' – excessive preoccupation with lucky/unlucky numbers, colours, days, etc.; avoiding stepping on cracks in the pavement or certain objects or places, due to unfounded beliefs about them.

This list is by no means exhaustive. For more examples of typical OCD behaviours and beliefs see chapter 1.

What to do when you suspect OCD

If you suspect that your partner, friend or family member may have obsessions or compulsions, try to broach the subject tactfully. It is important that you have a good understanding of the illness before you start the conversation.

How you can help

OCD affects not only the sufferer's life but also the lives of their family and friends, causing stress, frustration and anger. The most affected are usually people who live in the same household. It is only natural to try and help your loved one when you see them upset about something, so you offer to check, de-contaminate, or reassure them. However, OCD can spread like a wildfire, consuming the time and energy of other family members. Those who get involved in the vicious cycle of OCD, at some point, realise that the relief from the compulsion, ritual or reassurance is only temporary.

The role of family members, friends and carers

Support and help from people who care is invaluable in breaking the cycle of OCD. This is why NICE recommends that family members, friends and carers of OCD sufferers should be involved in the treatment process, if appropriate.

Get informed

Knowledge is power, so try to gather as much information as you need to understand the illness. This book is just one of many guides on OCD. Search your local library catalogue for more or check the list of recommended readings and websites at the end of this book.

A number of charities provide support to people suffering from anxiety disorders, and OCD in particular. Some of them (e.g. OCD-UK) also offer support to the families and carers. See the list at the end of the book for more details.

'If you suspect that your partner, friend or family member may have obsessions or compulsions, try to broach the subject tactfully. It is important that you have a good understanding of the illness before you start the conversation.'

Get involved in the care

This book can provide you with a general knowledge about the illness, but it cannot replace medical advice. If you are actively involved in caring for a person with OCD, the best way of understanding their particular situation and treatment is to accompany your loved one to their appointments with their health care professional. Ask the person you care for if you can go with them to see their GP, psychiatrist, or therapist. You should be given information about the treatments, possible side effects, how to identify risks (e.g. suicidal intent), and how to best deal with the illness. This can also be a great opportunity to ask about support groups, voluntary organisations and support for yourself.

'There is no direct link between parenting style or family stressors and the onset of OCD, so don't blame yourself for causing the illness.'

Don't blame yourself

As discussed in chapter 2, there is no direct link between parenting style or family stressors and the onset of OCD, so don't blame yourself for causing the illness.

You should not feel guilty for not being able to identify OCD symptoms earlier either – it is a secretive illness and the beginnings are often benign. Being thorough, neat, well organised and morally sound are appreciated in our society.

Understand the illness

Symptoms of OCD can be irrational and frustrating, and they seem like that to the sufferer too. Try to remember that despite being aware of the futility of the rituals, the person still feels compelled by the illness to perform the behaviours, and is coping the best way they can.

Criticism and negative comments don't help either. A person with OCD can't just 'pull themselves together' and stop the behaviours. Try to focus on the positive aspects of your loved one's life, praise successes at resisting the illness and encourage further attempts at challenging their OCD.

Help them to get help

It may take a while for the sufferer to acknowledge that they have OCD, and sometimes a while longer to accept the fact that they need help. Try to be understanding and empathetic. Encourage them to read about the illness – you may offer them educational materials directly, or leave them around the house in the hope they will pick it up and read it of their own accord.

Praise successes and encourage

Breaking free from obsessive-compulsive disorder may be a long battle. Your support along the way is invaluable. Praise your loved one's successes and celebrate achievements. Remember, it often takes a while before you can see the first benefits of the treatment, so your encouragement to carry on with taking the medication and attending the therapy sessions will be very important.

Dealing with reassurance seeking and rituals

Families and friends often get involved in rituals or obsessive reassurance seeking, mainly because they want to help their loved ones and this way feels natural and initially simple. Sometimes, even though they feel it is not the right thing to do, they don't know how else they can alleviate the sufferer's stress. They may also just go along with what the illness dictates for the sake of 'keeping the peace' and not upsetting the sufferer further.

Be constructively involved

As explained in chapter 2, providing reassurance and helping in rituals brings only temporary relief from anxiety. In the long run, this approach is not helpful and can actually maintain the cycle. Although it may seem harsh and counter-intuitive, say 'no' to OCD. Try not to give reassurance, don't get involved in checking, cleaning or other rituals.

Encourage the sufferer to challenge their beliefs, expose themselves to worrying thoughts or fearful situations. Support their efforts to continue with the treatment, particularly if they are struggling with ERP.

'Say 'no' to OCD. Try not to give reassurance, don't get involved in checking, cleaning or other rituals.'

Looking after yourself

As a carer, you put the person you care for first, which is great, but you can't forget about your own needs. If you don't make sure you are well and happy, your energy to support your loved one in their battle with OCD will suffer. Make sure that you look after yourself.

Have a healthy lifestyle

You don't have to make big changes - just make sure that you have a healthy lifestyle.

Here is a list of tips on how to look after yourself:

- Eat healthily and regularly, drink plenty of fluids, particularly water; avoid too much tea, coffee or alcohol.
- Keep fit - you don't have to go to the gym three times a week, but make sure that you take regular exercise adjusted to your level of fitness.
- Keep an eye on your stress levels. Learn how to recognise and manage stress in a positive way.
- Make sure you sleep enough and have rest and regular breaks.
- Pay attention to your own needs and make sure you have time for yourself.
- Don't be afraid to ask for help and support when you need it.
- Talk to someone you trust or find a support group for carers.

Am I entitled to any benefits?

If you are a UK resident aged 16 or over and caring for someone ill or disabled for at least 35 hours a week, you may be entitled to Carer's Allowance. Check www.direct.gov.uk and the section 'Caring for someone' for more details.

Need support and more information?

If you need support or more information on OCD or caring for someone with the illness, check the last section of this book. You will find contact details and short information on charities and other organisations which help people affected by mental health problems, and OCD in particular. Their websites often have sections for carers - this is an excellent starting point to finding the information and support you need.

You can also ask at the clinic that your loved one attends if they run a group for carers. If you can't find anything face-to-face, search the Internet. OCD-UK website is a good place to find addresses of support groups for carers of OCD sufferers. There are also other fora, like OCD forum (www.ocdforums.org), or Stuck In a Doorway (www.stuckinadoorway.org) where families and friends of OCD sufferers can seek information and support.

More on being a carer

Carers UK (www.carersuk.org) is a UK organisation providing free information and support by carers for carers.

The Need2Know book *'Caring - The Essential Guide'* contains valuable information on different aspects of being a carer.

Summing Up

Being a carer for someone suffering from OCD is a challenging job. Daily struggles to get through simple tasks, stresses of running late or not being able to go somewhere, putting life on hold because of the endless rituals – it's all part of that. Your role in the battle with the illness is important, so get armed with knowledge about OCD and understanding of your loved one's specific difficulties.

It's often carers who help OCD sufferers make their first step towards recovery, and then support them through the treatment. But don't let OCD take over your own life and sanity – say 'no' to reassurance seeking and rituals.

Remember, recovery from OCD is a long journey with ups and downs along the way, so make sure you don't forget about your own needs during the struggle. Take care of yourself.

Chapter Six

Young People and OCD

Young people get OCD too

OCD can begin at any age and any stage of life. Studies show that it often starts in childhood or adolescence, and can be diagnosed in children as young as 4-5 years old. Although symptoms are similar to those experienced by adults, OCD in young people may go undetected or misdiagnosed, not only because children are good at hiding their symptoms, but because they often don't recognise they have a problem. Their ability to explain what they are experiencing can be affected by their developmental stage. It is therefore important that the diagnosis of OCD is made by a professional with knowledge and experience, not only of mental disorders, but also awareness of age specific difficulties (e.g. CAMHS teams - Child and Adolescent Community Mental Health Services).

OCD in young people, and accompanying problems

Unfortunately, young people often have other psychological problems which develop as a consequence of OCD. Studies have shown that children and adolescents with OCD are more likely to suffer from generalised anxiety, separation anxiety, struggle with social situations or have difficulty managing their anger. These accompanying conditions need to be taken into account during assessment and treatment.

OCD – a brief guide for young people

What is OCD?

OCD is an illness where people spend a lot of time worrying over and over again about the same things. They also do things repeatedly, like wash their hands or check if the door is locked, because they feel their hands are not clean enough, or the door is not properly locked. People who suffer from OCD are often 'obsessed' with routines and doing things the same way every time. For example, when they are doing their homework, they always do maths first, then science, then English. Their books must be arranged in alphabetical order, or from the biggest to the smallest, etc. They feel they have to do it this way, because if they change their routine something bad will happen to them or their loved ones.

> 'Children are naturally "obsessed" with routines and rituals, because it's a good way to feel safe and contained. This is nothing to worry about, because most young people grow out of it.'

Sneaky illness

The unhealthy routines and worries take up a lot of time. Some OCD sufferers struggle with their jobs or schoolwork. They may not have time for their family or friends, or just for fun. OCD is a sneaky illness which, if untreated, can eat away at their lives.

Young people and routines

Children are naturally 'obsessed' with routines and rituals, because it's a good way to feel safe and contained. This is nothing to worry about, because most young people grow out of it.

Do I have OCD?

If you worry too much about lucky and unlucky numbers, catching germs, hurting someone, or that something bad may happen to you, your family or friends, you may have OCD. You may also have it if you spend a lot of time checking and rechecking things, washing your hands, changing clothes, counting or repeating 'lucky phrases' in your head.

If you are suffering from any of the described symptoms, talk to your parents or any other trusted family member, your teacher or the school nurse. They may suggest that you need to see your doctor, the best person to tell (diagnose) if you're suffering from OCD.

Remember, OCD is an illness, like asthma or eczema, and should be treated.

Visiting the doctor

When you go to see your doctor, he or she will talk to you to find out if you have OCD. There is no test or scan to check if you have it, so it is important that you try to answer your doctor's questions as honestly and thoroughly as you can. Try not to feel ashamed or guilty - OCD is not your fault. It's an illness which affects about 2% of young people. This means that if your school has 1,000 pupils, about 20 of them may have OCD. You are not alone with your problem.

Is there any help?

The doctor will explain the diagnosis to you and your parents (or any other adult accompanying you), and talk about treatments. Most likely you will be referred for a treatment called cognitive behaviour therapy, (CBT for short), or exposure and response prevention (ERP). Don't worry about the long, complicated names - you can use the letters, call it 'my treatment' or find your own name for it.

CBT and ERP are types of therapy. Therapy is a kind of training, where you will learn how to fight your worries and challenge your unhealthy routines. Your mum or dad, or even the entire family if necessary, will also be involved in helping you face up to your problems.

If you are really struggling, your doctor may also offer you a medication, which will help you deal with your anxiety.

Want to know more?

If you would like to know more about OCD, you may ask your doctor or your parents for advice regarding further readings. OCD-UK produce easy-to-read leaflets on obessive-compulsive disorder prepared with children and young people in mind. You can find these documents on their website www.ocduk.org by clicking on 'Children's Guide' or 'Teen's Guide' depending on your age.

'Younger children are more likely to be obsessed with "special" or "lucky" numbers, or other elements of magical thinking, like their powers to control events in the world.'

For parents and carers

OCD symptoms and development

OCD symptoms can affect a young sufferer's social, educational and emotional development. It is crucial that the illness is diagnosed and treated as soon as possible.

OCD can affect other aspects of a young person's life

OCD symptoms in young people have a tendency to become generalised and 'spread' over several areas of life. This causes further psychological and emotional problems. Many children with OCD struggle with schoolwork, separation anxiety, social anxiety or anger management.

Child's age and manifestation of OCD

Mental and emotional development can also affect the way the OCD is manifested. Younger children are more likely to be obsessed with 'special' or 'lucky' numbers, or other elements of magical thinking, like their powers to control events in the world. Older children and teenagers may focus more on moral codes, religion and, of course, homework.

Children and rituals

Rituals and routines are integral parts of many children's lives, and often beneficial in helping them feel safe and contained. A perfect example of a good ritual is a bedtime routine. Sometimes, even minor disturbances to those routines may bring on a major temper tantrum, as many toddlers' parents can certify. These rituals are common between the ages of two and eight.

As the child grows their repetitive behaviours change. He or she often starts collecting sports cards, dolls, comic books, jewellery, etc. Some young people engage in highly ritualised and rule-bound games or 'obsessive' preoccupations with a sport or music idol. These are all normal stages of a healthy development, which help young people deal with their fears and control their environment. As new coping strategies develop, these behaviours disappear.

'Rituals and routines are common between the ages of two and eight.'

When do rituals become a problem?

You should seek professional advice if your child's rituals persist past adolescence, become more and more rigid and disabling, or if attempts at stopping them result in extreme anxiety. Don't hesitate to speak to your doctor or other health care professional if your child's behaviour worries you in any other way.

See chapter 5 for advice on caring for someone with OCD.

Typical symptoms

OCD in young people follows similar patterns as adult OCD. Children and teenagers may worry about germs, safety, harm, order or cleanliness. They may perform rituals and other compulsions in the same way as adults do. However, very often, symptoms experienced by your child will be related to their developmental stage so, for example, younger children may be preoccupied with toys, 'magical thinking', body wastes and family members, while older ones - with homework, germs and friends.

Common OCD signs

Your child may be suffering from OCD if she/he:

- Keeps their room very tidy and insists on having their toys/books/ornaments in a certain order or neatly aligned and any disruption to the order causes her/him distress.
- Can react with unexpected anger or upset if a usual routine is interrupted.
- Needs to wash their hands or have a shower/bath very often.
- Avoids 'messy' play or art/science projects.
- Needs to repeat certain numbers or count to a certain number.
- Is preoccupied with 'safe', 'lucky' or 'bad' numbers or words.
- Spends a lot of time making sure their homework is perfect, checking, rechecking and rewriting it until it becomes 'perfect'; you may even notice holes erased in their workbooks.
- Is often late for school, stays up longer to complete assignments, stays home from school.
- Worries a lot about harm or danger that may happen to their parents, siblings etc.
- Often seeks reassurance regarding their health and wellbeing.
- Finds it hard to part with old, broken toys, packaging or other seemingly unnecessary items.

- Feels an urge to repeatedly check locks, taps, windows, etc.

- Spends a lot of time getting ready in the morning or for bed at nighttime.

- Repeatedly requests that you or other family members answer the same question or repeat strange phrases.

This list is by no means exhaustive. If you are concerned that your child is suffering from OCD, do not hesitate to seek professional advice.

Help! My child has OCD

Seeking help for your child

If you're seeking help for your child, your GP is usually the best person to talk to in the first instance. They may decide to refer your child to a specialist service, such as Child and Adolescent Mental Health Services (CAMHS).

If your child is young, it is natural that you will do it on their behalf. However, older children, and particularly teenagers, may want to speak to their doctor themselves. In any case, you may need to accompany your child to support and encourage them.

'Older children, and particularly teenagers may want to speak to their doctor themselves.'

Don't blame yourself

Seeing your child suffer may be heartbreaking and many parents feel guilty about not being able to do much about it. Some may even blame themselves for somehow causing OCD. Remember, OCD is an illness which, although may be brought on by life events or stress, is not a simple cause-effect scenario and there are several factors at play. In a nutshell - parents do not cause OCD.

For more information on what causes OCD and how it develops see chapter 1 and 2. If you have any doubts or questions, ask your child's doctor or therapist.

OCD, young people and their families

Parents and families of young OCD sufferers are affected by the illness and often get involved in rituals. On the other hand, families can be a great source of support for young people and play an important role in the recovery process.

Get actively involved in the treatment

Treatment for OCD requires a good understanding of the illness and a lot of motivation to keep challenging the symptoms. Therapy is a tough job and patience is crucial when medication is concerned. Your encouragement and support is essential to your child's triumph over the illness. Get actively involved in the treatment. Speak to your child's doctor, therapist or another member of the team about your role and how you can best help your child.

What treatment is available?

OCD symptoms in adults and young people are similar, follow similar patterns and have similar themes. They also respond to similar treatment. However, it needs to be adapted to the child's specific needs and take developmental differences into consideration.

As in adults, there are two main groups of treatment recommended for OCD in young people: psychological interventions and medication.

As previously noted, treatment should take into consideration co-existing problems, like generalised anxiety or anger management issues.

Psychological treatments

NICE guidance recommends that your child should be offered psychological approach as first-line treatment.

Family involvement

Despite many similarities with adults, OCD symptoms in young people are reflective of the stage your child is at developmentally and almost always involve the family. This is why any psychoeducation and treatment need to be age-appropriate, and ideally involve the family. Psychological interventions for OCD have been adapted to suit the needs and abilities of young people, and include their families.

Parents' and families' involvement in CBT and ERP enhance the child's chances at succeeding in breaking free from OCD.

CBT (cognitive behavioural therapy)

The best 'talking therapy' for OCD in children and young adults is CBT. This is an approach which helps the young person understand how their thoughts, feelings and actions are connected and influence one another. It also teaches how to challenge unhelpful beliefs and deal with upsetting thoughts.

Similarly to adults, the guided self-help in the CBT approach may be enough to help the young person overcome their difficulties. If it fails, or the symptoms are more problematic, a referral to secondary services and more intense CBT (including ERP) is required. It usually involves 10-20 weekly sessions, one-to-one with a therapist or in family settings. It may also be useful to involve the school to enhance the beneficial effects and rally more support.

ERP (exposure and response prevention)

ERP is part of CBT treatment. It focuses on encouraging the young sufferer to face their fears and challenge their urges to carry out rituals in a structured and supportive environment. Young people are never forced to do anything beyond their ability to cope.

ERP is the treatment where family participation and support is most valued and has been found to improve the outcome.

General rules regarding engagement in talking therapies and

'Parents' and families' involvement in CBT and ERP enhance the child's chances at succeeding in breaking free from OCD.'

CBT in particular

Although CBT and ERP are adapted to suit the needs and developmental stage of young people, many of the general rules regarding the choice of therapist and therapeutic engagement still apply. See chapters 3 and 4 for general information on these processes.

Your doctor or therapist should be able to give you a detailed explanation of what your therapy will consists of, how long it is going to take and other 'ground rules'. Don't be afraid of asking questions if you have any.

Family focused interventions

At the moment there is no evidence that family therapy or family interventions aimed at changing the family functioning decrease the symptoms of OCD. However, family therapy may be helpful in improving communication and resolving additional problems.

Cognitive therapy

Some young people may find the cognitive approach useful, but there is still not enough evidence to recommend this method in the treatment of OCD in young people

Other psychological approaches

Psychotherapy, anxiety management or other psychological approaches have not been found beneficial in challenging OCD symptoms. However, they may be offered to help young people overcome other accompanying difficulties.

Medication

Although medication is not recommended as first-line treatment for young people, there are situations when the doctor will consider prescribing it.

What medication can be prescribed to young people?

The medication used to treat OCD in young people is similar to those used for adults. NICE recommends that in cases of poor response to CBT or if there are co-existing problems, an SSRI or clomipramine can be prescribed. The drug will go hand in hand with the therapy.

Medication can be as effective as CBT in reducing the symptoms and their impact on the young person's life. Potential risks of side effects and other unknown effects on the developing nervous system, need to be taken into consideration before prescribing as well.

You will find more general information about the medication used in OCD and prescribing in chapter 3.

If you have any questions or concerns regarding your medication, do not hesitate to ask your doctor.

PANDAS (Paediatric Autoimmune Neuropsychiatric Disorder Associated with Streptococcus)

Childhood onset of OCD has been linked to infection with a bacteria, which causes Strep throat (Streptococcus). It is believed that the antibodies produced by the organism to kill the bacteria can also interact with the brain tissue and trigger or worsen the OCD symptoms. This is a rare condition and children with Strep-related OCD respond very well to antibiotics used to treat the infection.

Summing Up

Obessive-compulsive disorder in children and young people shares many similarities with adult OCD. The symptoms follow the same themes and patterns, families often get involved in compulsive acts and reassurance, the same treatments in age-appropriate adaptations are recommended, but young people often come across more challenges. They struggle to express what they are experiencing. There is a higher chance of them having additional psychological problems co-existing and deriving from OCD. Their OCD symptoms interfere with their social, educational and emotional development. It is therefore important that OCD in young people is diagnosed and treated as soon as possible to stop the illness invading more and more of the young person's life.

Chapter Seven

OCD and Company

OCD is one of the most common psychiatric problems, affecting around 2-3% of the population. Unfortunately, OCD sufferers are more likely to struggle with additional mental health conditions, which are often consequences of OCD.

There are also a number of other disorders described as being on the, so-called, OCD spectrum. These conditions involve experiencing repetitive thoughts or behaviours, but are not strictly-speaking obsessive-compulsive.

OCD spectrum disorders

Some researchers believe that the nature of OCD symptoms suggests that this illness is related to other disorders, which involve stereotyped and repetitive thoughts or behaviours.

Tics and Tourette's Syndrome

Tourette's Syndrome is a neurological disorder characterised by repeated bouts of involuntary movements (e.g. eye blinking, grimacing, tapping) or vocalisations (e.g. grunting, using offensive words, throat clearing). These behaviours are called tics. They often increase with stress and tension and decrease when the person is relaxed or absorbed in a task.

Like in OCD, a tics sufferer cannot resist the unwanted urge to release the behaviours, and the relief which follows is also only temporary. Although some genetic and family studies show that a significant proportion of people with tics also suffer from OCD, no clear link between these conditions has been found so far.

OCD and tics respond to different treatments.

'There are also a number of other disorders described as being on the so-called OCD spectrum. These conditions involve repetitive thoughts or behaviours, but are not strictly-speaking obsessive-compulsive.'

Compulsive hair-pulling (trichotillomania)

Trichotillomania is a psychological condition in which people affected feel repeated, irresistible urges to pull their hair out. This problem develops often in adolescents or young adults, mainly females, varies in severity and in extreme cases may result in baldness. Pulling can occur at any part of the body and most often involves scalp, eyebrows and eyelashes, beard or pubic area. Hair-pulling is preceded by an increasing sense of tension and the behaviour brings relief, satisfaction or even pleasure.

Compulsive hair-pulling is an impulse control disorder, and is usually treated with another type of CBT – habit reversal training, medication and/or education.

Compulsive skin-picking (CSP)

Compulsive skin picking (dermatillomania, neurotic excoriation) is another impulse control behaviour, similar to trichotillomania. It involves habitual and excessive picking of normal variations of healthy skin (like freckles and moles), lesions (acne blemishes or scabs) or even imagined skin defects. This behaviour most often affects the face, but can involve any part of the body and result in bleeding, bruises, infection and often disfigurement of the sufferer's skin.

Compulsive skin-picking often co-exists with OCD and body dysmorphic disorder (BDD). Picking may be preceded by high levels of tension and an urge and followed by feelings of relief or pleasure.

CSP responds to CBT and habit reversal training in particular.

Hypochondria (hypochondriasis, health anxiety)

Hypochondria is an obsessional fear of having a serious medical condition. People affected by it misinterpret common symptoms, like headache, cough or minor sore throat as signs of brain tumour, lung cancer or AIDS, for example.

Treatment for hypochondria includes SSRIs and CBT.

Obsessive-compulsive personality disorder

Obsessive-compulsive personality disorder (OCPD) and OCD share many features and some theories argue that OCPD predisposes to OCD, or that OCPD is 'on the spectrum'. However, there is little evidence as yet to prove these links.

For more information on OCPD see chapter 1.

Other repetitive behaviours

There are many other repetitive behaviours, which have been labelled incorrectly as 'obsessive' or 'compulsive'. Examples include, compulsive shopping, gambling or other addictions; as well as being obsessed with someone or something.

For more examples and information on what is and what is not OCD, see chapter 1.

OCD and depression

Depression is not related to OCD but it often affects OCD sufferers and further complicates the picture of the illness. Although depression often develops as a direct result of OCD, it needs to be diagnosed and treated in its own right, alongside OCD.

'Depression often develops as a direct result of OCD, however it needs to be diagnosed and treated in its own right, alongside OCD.'

This section looks only at the basic features of depression to help you identify its symptoms. For more information about depression see another Need2Know title: *Depression – the Essential Guide*.

What is depression?

Depression is one of the most common mental health problems, affecting millions of people every day around the world. It is more than just feeling down. Depressive symptoms are present nearly every day for most of the day and usually are not responsive to circumstances.

Depressive symptoms

You may be depressed if in the past two weeks you have experienced at least two of the following symptoms:

- Feeling low, down, sad.

- Having mood swings, getting angry or irritated over little things.

- Feeling worthless, incompetent or guilty.

- Having reduced energy, getting tried easily.

- Having problems with your sleep (e.g. trouble falling asleep, waking up frequently, or waking up early and not being able to get back to sleep; you may also sleep more than usual).

- Experiencing changes in your appetite (e.g. poor appetite or overeating), resulting in weight loss and/or gain.

- Loss of interest in activities you normally enjoy.

- Struggling to do your daily chores, even to take care of your own appearance, hygiene or the cleanliness of your house.

- Having a bleak or pessimistic view of the future.

- Experiencing ideas of self-harm or suicide.

This list is not exhaustive and is not intended as a diagnostic tool. If you feel you may be suffering from depression, seek professional help. Your GP is the best first step – he/she will be able to diagnose your condition properly and suggest suitable treatment.

Treatment

Treatment of depression depends on the severity of the symptoms, the context in which the illness developed and personal circumstances. Most often it includes antidepressant medications, counselling, CBT or other talking therapies, light therapy, healthy lifestyle adjustments or a combination of these.

OCD and anxiety

Anxiety is a normal emotion. When you face a threatening situation, your mind is focused on it and your body goes into the 'fight or flight' mode with your heart racing, your breathing becoming faster, your muscles getting tense and shaking. When the threat ceases, your body also calms down and goes back into its natural, more relaxed mode. These reactions are common to all humans (and also to some animals), and evolved as a defence mechanism.

Unfortunately, sometimes these natural protections get out of proportion to the threat or last for longer than the stressful situation and anxiety becomes a problem. Anxiety disorders are very common with as many as one in every 10 people suffering from them.

Types of anxiety disorders

Anxiety disorders can be divided into two groups, depending on how the symptoms occur in time:

- Continuous anxiety – when symptoms are present most of the time (like it is in generalised anxiety disorder).
- Episodic anxiety, with symptoms being limited in time and often specific to the situation (e.g. phobias, panic attacks).

Anxiety symptoms

Symptoms of anxiety are common to all types of anxiety disorders. They may be of a psychological or physical nature and vary from individual to individual and can change with time. The most common anxiety symptoms are:

- Worrying.
- Fearful anticipation.
- Sensitivity to noise.
- Poor concentration.
- Irritability.

- Dry mouth.

- Lump in the throat or difficulty swallowing.

- Frequent or loose bowel motions.

- Difficulty breathing.

- Palpitations.

- Discomfort in the chest.

- Tremors or shaking.

- Dizziness.

- Headache.

- Insomnia, night terrors or other difficulties sleeping.

If you are concerned about any of these symptoms, talk to your doctor or your therapist about it.

For more information on anxiety, see Need2Know: *Anxiety - The Essential Guide*.

Anxiety Disorder or OCD?

Anxiety is an integral part of OCD, but here these symptoms occur in relation to distressing thoughts or images and are temporarily resolved by rituals. On the other hand, people suffering from other anxiety disorders can sometimes develop obsessional symptoms, which are usually milder than in OCD.

As you can see, other anxiety disorders and OCD can sometimes present in a similar way, however, as the treatment for OCD differs from the other conditions, it is important that your doctor understands your problem and diagnoses it correctly. Remember, you are the best person to explain what is going on for you, so be honest and as thorough as possible.

'Other anxiety disorders and OCD can sometimes present in a similar way, however, as the treatment for OCD differs from the other conditions, it is important that your doctor understands your problem and diagnoses it correctly.'

OCD and psychosis

Many OCD sufferers worry that their illness may lead to a psychosis (or more specifically, schizophrenia). Although people with psychosis may experience unwanted, strange thoughts or thoughts revolving around violence, religious or sexual themes, OCD is an essentially different and completely unrelated illness.

What is psychosis?

Psychosis is a type of mental illness characterised by delusions (beliefs not based in reality) and/or hallucinations (hearing noises or voices when there is no one around, seeing or smelling things that are not there). People who suffer from psychosis often have difficulty in expressing their thoughts and feelings and their speech may come across as strange or nonsensical.

Treatment

Psychosis is treated with antipsychotic medication and sometimes a special type of CBT or other therapies.

It is important to emphasise that suffering from OCD does not increase your risk of developing psychosis or schizophrenia. If you have any doubts, ask your doctor or health professional for advice.

'OCD does not increase your risk of developing psychosis or schizophrenia.'

OCD and substance misuse

OCD symptoms, whether obsessions, compulsions or anxiety, are unpleasant. Some sufferers may resort to using alcohol or illegal drugs to forget about their illness or reduce the intensity of their symptoms. This is dangerous for a number of reasons. First of all, these substances do not treat your OCD, they only mask the symptoms, which are back the moment the effects of the substance wears off. Harmful use of substances may lead to dependency, addictions and many other mental and general health problems. If you are on anti-OCD medication and drinking or using drugs, be aware that these combinations can cause further problems. This is particularly the case with alcohol.

Even if you use alcohol in moderate amounts, read the medication information leaflet or speak to your GP about it.

Body dysmorphic disorder – obsessed with ugliness?

Body dysmorphic disorder (dysmorphophobia, BDD) is an anxiety disorder in which the sufferer is preoccupied with an imagined or minor defect in their appearance. These obsessions can be related to any part of their body, but most commonly are focused on the person's face, thinning hair, acne, asymmetry or disproportion of body features (e.g. breasts, genitals, feet, etc.). Sometimes, the complaints are vague and concerned with perceived generalised ugliness.

These beliefs may become so fixed and firm that they reach the level of delusions.

As a result of their thoughts, the sufferers spend a lot of time checking the appearance of the concerned body part, trying to 'fix' the defect by camouflage, or seek cosmetic or dermatological treatments. They often compare the appearance of the perceived defects with that of others and avoid social or intimate situations for the fear of the flaw being exposed or because of embarrassment.

Typical BDD symptoms

The most typical symptoms of BDD are:

- Strong concerns that a body part is flawed, asymmetrical or disproportionate, despite the environment (family, friends, health professionals) testifying to the contrary.

- Spending a lot of time in front of a mirror checking the perceived flaw.

- Putting a lot of time and effort into camouflaging the defect with make-up, clothing or excessive grooming.

- Dieting and excessive exercise.

- Comparing the appearance of the concerned part of the body with others and seeking reassurance.

- Avoidance of social and intimate situations because of the embarrassment or low self-esteem related to the perceived ugliness.

- Seeking dermatological treatment and cosmetic surgery, despite being told it is not necessary.

Onset of BDD

BDD usually starts in adolescence and early adulthood when people are generally sensitive about their appearance. Milder symptoms can resolve with time, but in more severe situations, if untreated, BDD can significantly affect the sufferer's life, leading to social isolation, unemployment and suicide attempts.

Treatment

The treatment recommended for body dysmorphic disorder by NICE is similar to OCD and includes CBT with ERP; and antidepressants from the group of SSRIs (fluoxetine is probably more effective than others). These interventions can be used separately or in combination, depending on the severity of the symptoms. Sometimes augmentation with an antipsychotic medication may be required.

If you suspect you may suffer from BDD speak to your GP.

Summing Up

Some researchers believe that OCD belongs to a family of disorders characterised by repetitive and stereotyped symptoms. They talk about an 'OCD spectrum' which includes tics, compulsive skin-picking, hair-pulling or obsessive-compulsive personality disorder. Body dysmorphic disorder is another condition with symptoms and treatment similar to OCD.

On top of their struggle with obsessive thoughts and compulsive behaviours, OCD sufferers are often affected by other mental health conditions, most commonly depression, anxiety and substance misuse. If you think you may suffer from any of the aforementioned conditions, speak to your doctor.

Chapter Eight

Living with OCD

Getting well

The road to your recovery starts with the very first step - recognising that you have a problem and asking for help. If you haven't seen your doctor about your OCD yet, book an appointment as soon as possible. Give yourself a chance to get well.

Early diagnosis is vital

OCD is an illness that, if not treated, can take over your life. Due to the shame and embarrassment, which often accompany OCD, sufferers are reluctant to seek help. Sometimes, the symptoms get so bad and overwhelming, the person is unable to leave the house and becomes a prisoner of their own bedroom or bathroom. This situation may carry on for a long time, with the sufferer being trapped in a vicious cycle of obsessions, rituals and endless repetitions. This is why it is crucial that you seek appropriate help as soon as possible

Case Study

Rob: 'I can't remember anymore when it all first started, but I certainly remember when I first realised something was wrong. It was on the day I lost my job, as I had missed yet another deadline. At the time, I was already working from home because of my rituals and spending hours checking, rechecking and correcting my work on the computer. I couldn't sleep because my mind wouldn't stop thinking about possible errors and their consequences. My work colleagues would hang up when I rang them seeking reassurance and asking the same questions over and over again.

'At the time I was so concentrated on getting things done I couldn't see I was already very unwell. I thought I needed to work harder. I felt isolated and lonely but still carried on as if everything was OK. I'd always thought I was just one of those talented geeks - maybe not very good at everyday life, but a real whiz when it came to my work. The job loss was like a bucket of cold water poured over my head. It took me a couple more days to realise that my problems weren't related to my confidence. It was OCD. I finally I rang my GP for help.'

Be patient

Overcoming your OCD will take time. The medication takes a few weeks to fully develop its anti-OCD properties and it is not unusual to wait a couple of months to see if it's working for you. Most people who regularly attend their weekly session of CBT or ERP will see the benefits of the therapy after 12-20 sessions. It is important that you are patient and stay motivated. If you worry about your slow progress, talk to your doctor or your therapist.

Keep motivated

Whether it is about seeing your progress in therapy or waiting for the medication to take effect, don't lose hope. Remember that getting well takes time. Remind yourself that the ultimate goal of your journey is your freedom from OCD symptoms and having your life back.

Keep your goal in focus

Put your goal in writing and stick little reminders in various places in your home: the refrigerator door, or a bathroom mirror, so you can see and read them as often as possible. You can even make a banner and put it up to read it every time you feel like you may give in.

Imagine your personal, professional and social life without OCD - visualise it and write it down using as many specifics as possible.

Some people find listening more useful than reading or writing - if that's the case, just record your visualisations on a tape (CD, mp3) and listen to it as often as you need.

Rally support

Ask your family or friends to join you on your road to recovery. They may become involved on many different levels - from providing day-to-day support, through to disengaging from rituals, or even becoming actively involved in your therapy. Talk to your therapist or your doctor how you can make the most of the support from your family and friends.

Remember, OCD affects one in every 50 people, so you are not alone in your battle with the illness. Find a support group in your area - ask at your clinic, check OCD-UK, Royal College of Psychiatrists' websites or the last section of this book for some suggestions.

If, for whatever reason, you struggle to access face-to-face support, join in an online group or forum. Many mental health-related charities list trusted sites, provide newsletters or message boards, have chat rooms or an 'Ask our Expert' option.

Track and celebrate your progress

Tracking your progress will help you see where on the road to recovery you are. This may be part of your therapy or you may wish to do it just for yourself. You can do it in whatever form you want - a diary, a series of reports or a chart. It is useful to have a good account of your 'entry point', listing the amount of time consumed by your obsessional thoughts and rituals, or the extent to which OCD symptoms affected your life (e.g. you were unable to work, you were housebound, or you couldn't play with your children).

Try to keep track of your progress in regular intervals so you can compare where you are and where you were, e.g. last week. Be mindful that checking your progress too often, e.g. every day, may not reflect the improvements as the changes may be too small for you to notice.

Don't forget to celebrate your successes, however minor they may seem - they are steps on your way to freedom from OCD symptoms.

Helping yourself

The first, and most important thing you can do to help yourself is to seek help as soon as you realise your life is affected by unpleasant, intrusive thoughts and compulsive behaviours. You don't have to know the name for those thoughts and behaviours.

Rob (see the case study at the beginning of this chapter) spent a couple of days reading up on OCD and taking and retaking self-check tests, 'just to make sure' and 'double check'. You don't need to make sure it is OCD before you ask for help. Talk to your doctor - he or she will know how to diagnose your problem. Tell them about your difficulties, describe how it affects your everyday life, give examples. Be open and honest. You are not the first person to disclose these sorts of problems to them. Try not to feel embarrassed or ashamed - OCD is not your fault, it is an illness and as such needs to be treated.

10 things you can do to help yourself

Once you know that your problem is OCD, you can start appropriate treatment. Breaking free from OCD may take a long time, but don't lose your spirit. There are a number of things you can do to encourage your recovery:

- Treat your OCD as an obstacle to living your life and being happy - fight it!

- Don't blame yourself for having OCD. Be kind to yourself.

- Follow your doctor's advice regarding medication.

- Attend your therapy sessions regularly and follow your therapist's guidance.

- Don't hesitate, feel embarrassed or ashamed to ask your doctor or therapist any questions.

- Gather support from health professionals, your family, friends, support groups (see the last section of this book for more information).

- Read up on OCD - books, trusted websites (check the last section of this book for recommendations), leaflets. Get some self-help materials. The better you know your opponent, the more successful you will be at fighting it.

- Follow the ERP rules in everyday life: expose yourself to your obsessive thoughts and resist the rituals.

- Don't use alcohol or other substances to control your anxiety. Try to lead a healthy life.

- Be patient and stay motivated. It may take a while to break free from OCD but it is worth it - you'll have your life back eventually.

Coping with lapses and relapses

Lapses

These are episodes milder than the original illness in nature, short or time-limited and almost always related to life stresses, like moving house, changing jobs, physical illness. Sometimes even a happy event, like a birth of a baby or getting married may bring on a little 'OCD hiccup'. If this is the case, don't panic - it's normal or even natural. Your symptoms should subside soon and you will be able to return to your previous level of functioning.

Relapses

Relapses are part of recovery in any mental illness including OCD. This is why relapse prevention should be an important part of your treatment.

'Relapses are part of recovery in any mental illness including OCD. This is why relapse prevention should be an important part of your treatment.'

As many people experience a relapse of their OCD symptoms following coming off the medication, never stop your medication without consulting with your doctor.

Managing relapses

Relapses will happen, so be prepared. Do not see them as a sign of failure, but rather as opportunities to use the skills learned during your CBT/ERP course. It is good to keep your therapy notes handy.

It may also be helpful to have other ready-made tools to hand. You may want to invest in some self-help materials like *The OCD Workbook* by Hyman and Pedrick, or use the Four Steps Self-Help guide by Dr J. Schwartz provided free on OCD-UK website (go to www.ocduk.org then click on 'four steps self-help'). See the last section of this book for more recommendations.

Your rights

Living with a mental health problem can be a difficult experience not only because of the symptoms. Getting appropriate help and support are crucial, but sometimes difficult and treatment can be costly. You may find yourself unable to work, without any source of income or in a situation where you feel you are discriminated against because of your illness. It is therefore important that you know your rights.

Benefits

Unfortunately, OCD can affect your life to the extent that you may be unable to work temporarily or you could even lose your job completely. If your illness is affecting your ability to work, study or provide for yourself and your family, you may be eligible for some benefits.

The benefits available for people unable to work due to ill health changed in 2008 and they may still change in the coming years, so please refer to www.direct.gov.uk for up-to-date information.

At the time of writing this book the following benefits were available:

Employment and Support Allowance (ESA)

ESA is a financial help paid to people over 16 but before the state retirement pension age, who are unable to work because of an illness or disability.
An ESA also gives the person access to a personal advisor and a range of services to help manage their health problems at work and to prepare for work once they are capable of doing it.

Everyone claiming ESA will undergo a 13-week assessment period, at the end of which they have to go back to work or remain on the benefit either with a view to receiving further support towards returning to the workforce or not, depending on the outcome of the assessment.

Disability Living Allowance (DLA)

If your OCD is severe to the point that you have needed someone else's help or supervision to care for yourself or to maintain yours or others' safety for at least three months, and if this situation is likely to continue for at least six months, you may be eligible for DLA. You can get DLA whether you work or not.

Carer's Allowance

If you are over 16 years of age and spend at least 35 hours per week looking after someone in receipt of DLA, you may be eligible for Carer's Allowance.

See chapter 5 for more details on caring for someone with OCD.

Housing and Council Tax Benefits

If you are on a low income, you may be eligible for help with your rent (Housing Benefit) or council tax (Council Tax Benefit). For more details and to check if you are eligible, contact your local council.

This section of the book contains only very basic information on benefits available for people with mental illness. Please, see www.direct.gov.uk or www.rethink.org.uk for more information.

'If your illness is affecting your ability to work, study or provide for yourself and your family, you may be eligible for some benefits.'

Help with health costs

Most NHS care is free of charge, but you may need to pay for your medication, travel to and from your appointments or other services. If you are on Income Support, ESA or other income-related benefits, you may be entitled to free prescriptions and refunds to necessary travel costs to NHS appointments (as well as other services).

For more details visit the NHS Business Service Authority website: www. nhsbsa.nhs.uk and click on 'Help With Health Costs' button or ring their helpline - 0845 850 1166.

If you have to pay for four or more prescription items in three months, or more than 14 items in 12 months, a Prescription Prepayment Certificate (PPC) may be a cheaper option.

More information on this service is available on the NHS Business Service Authority website (www.nhsbsa.nhs.uk) in 'Help With Health Costs' and 'Prescription Prepayment Certificates' sections. You can also ring NHSBSA PPCs helpline - 0845 850 0030

Health care

As a lawful resident in the UK, you have a right to free health care under the National Health Service (NHS).

Your other health care-related rights include:

- Right to give or refuse consent to a treatment.
- Right to receive clear and understandable information about your health and treatment.
- Right to confidentiality - information about your illness, treatment, prognosis and other health-related matters should not be disclosed without your consent to anyone apart from the health professionals directly involved in your care.
- Right to access your health records.
- Right to duty of care - to receive care considered as appropriate to your condition.

For more details on your rights related to health care - go to www.rethink.org, click on 'Living with mental illness', then on 'Rights and laws' and browse through the Rethink selection of factsheet on rights and laws.

Equality Act and Disability Discrimination Act

Unfortunately, discrimination against people with mental illness is still a widespread problem and you may come across it in many areas of your life. In the UK the rights to services, facilities, education and employment for people with a disability, or other long-term physical or mental impairment are protected by The Equality Act (EA), which from October 2010 replaced the majority of The Disability Discrimination Act (DDA).

To know more about your rights under the EA and DDA check www.direct.gov.uk or www.rethink.org.

'In the UK the rights to services, facilities, education and employment for people with a disability, or other long-term physical or mental impairment are protected by The Equality Act, which from October 2010 replaced the majority of The Disability Discrimination Act.'

Summing Up

Living with OCD, like living with any mental illness is a challenge in itself, so make sure that you do everything you can to ensure your recovery and remain well. Get to know your rights and don't be afraid to use them to help you live with your illness. Motivation is crucial in maintaining your recovery and coping with minor hiccups and relapses, so get all the support you can rally. Don't forget to celebrate your progress. Whatever the stage of your recovery, stay clearly focused on your goals - breaking free from OCD is possible.

Chapter Nine

Moving On

Staying well

Getting well is only a part of your recovery. OCD is an illness that may return at any time. Around half of the people who come off their medication may experience a relapse, which is why it is important that every OCD sufferer receives CBT/ERP therapy, in whichever form is appropriate. CBT/ERP techniques will provide you with tools invaluable in challenging your symptoms at any moment and stage of your illness and life.

The rate of relapse for those who have been through therapy is lower than for those who have not been, but relapses still affect up to a quarter of sufferers.

WRAP

Many UK centres, particularly in secondary care (e.g. community mental health teams or outpatients' clinics) use a framework called WRAP (Wellness Recovery Action Plan), which was originally developed by Mary Ellen Copeland and a group of mental health service users. WRAP is a tool that promotes recovery, increased self-awareness, hope, stability and quality of life, as well as providing relapse prevention strategies.

WRAP is a personalised plan which takes time and effort to develop, but many people have found it beneficial on the road to getting and staying well. It can be used for any mental health condition and does not need to be prescribed.

Ask at your centre if they use WRAP or run WRAP-related groups etc., and how you could get involved in the process.

'Around half of the people who come off their medication may experience a relapse, which is why it is important that every OCD sufferer receives CBT/ERP therapy.'

You can also find more information on WRAP at Mary Ellen Copeland (www.mentalhealthrecovery.com) and Working Together For Recovery websites (www.workingtogetherforrecovery.co.uk) or any other recovery-orientated website.

Natural course of your illness

It is important to remember that OCD symptoms can wax and wane. There will be times in your life when your obsessions and compulsions may come back or become more prominent - this is part of the recovery process. In order to stay well you need to stay aware of OCD throughout your life.

Staying aware of your OCD

'A healthy mind in a healthy body.'

Roman poet, Juvenal

Having your eyes, ears and mind open to the possibility of the return of your OCD symptoms should help you identify even mild difficulties, so you can 'nip them in the bud', preventing further deterioration.

A healthy mind in a healthy body

Ancient Romans knew that our physical and emotional health are connected. For your mind to feel well, you need to feel well in your body. There are several books on healthy lifestyle and its different aspects available, so check your local library or a bookshop. You can also visit www.need2knowbooks.co.uk for some suggestions.

Remember, you don't need to make serious changes in your lifestyle to live healthier. Sometimes it's little things that make big differences.

Here are 10 basic rules for a healthy life:

1. Eat healthily.

2. Get adequate exercise.

3. Try to manage, or even reduce, stress.

4. Get enough rest and sleep.

5. Avoid alcohol and illegal drugs.

6. Have time for family and friends.

7. Have time for things you enjoy.

8. Find a good work/life balance.

9. Don't let OCD symptoms sneak back into your life - fill the time you used to spend on your rituals with work, exercises, old or new hobbies.

10. Try to be positive and enjoy your life.

Moving on

Although OCD is an illness that can take over your life and will not let you forget about it, this is not a reason why you should not have a normal life once the symptoms are under control.

Getting a life

Many OCD sufferers who manage to break free from the illness succeed at having a happy family, interesting social life and fulfilling careers. Establish what is important for you and set yourself achievable goals. Planning 'your life after and despite your OCD' may be part of your treatment and recovery plans.

Living with the stigma of a mental illness

Unfortunately, mental illness, including OCD, is still associated with social stigma and you may find yourself battling against discrimination and misunderstanding. If you feel you've been affected by stigma, speak to someone you trust or seek professional advice on how to address the issue.

You can also join in any of the anti-stigma campaigns. Rethink is a national charity dedicated to giving a voice to people affected by severe mental illness. You can read more about their work, goals and campaigns on their website: www.rethink.org

'Many OCD sufferers who manage to break free from the illness succeed at having a happy family, interesting social life and fulfilling careers.'

OCD and relationships

Many studies have found that people in relationships are generally happier and healthier. A recent large international study led by Dr Kate Scott from the University of Otago, New Zealand, showed that married people are less likely to suffer from mental disorders, including depression, anxiety or substance abuse. On the other hand, separation, divorce or the death of a spouse substantially increase the risk of mental health problems.

Good, trusting relationships, whether romantic or friendship-based can be invaluable sources of support and stability for you but aware that relationship difficulties may affect your mental state.

OCD affects relationships

As discussed in the previous chapters, family members and friends often get involved in the vicious cycle of OCD. On the other hand, they can also play an important role in the recovery.

When the worst part of the battle with your illness is behind you, it may be useful to sit with your partner and talk about ways your illness can affect your behaviour or mood and how it can further impact on your relationship. It is also important that your partner knows your illness, is able to recognise its signs and feels confident where and when to seek help. You may want to refer him or her to the appropriate chapters of this book or get them involved in conversations about early warning signs and a 'mental first aid kit' (see section on WRAP in this chapter).

Relationship problems can also affect the course of your OCD (see chapter 2 for details), so to minimise risks of a relapse try to learn how to recognise difficulties in your relationships early and deal with them.

Starting a family

Many young OCD sufferers worry if they will ever be able to have their own family. As you probably know by now, although OCD seems to 'run in families', there is no straightforward genetic link for it and evidence does not support suspicions that parents can pass their problems on to their children (see chapter 2 for details).

If you have any further questions about starting a family, speak to your doctor.

If you are on medication for your OCD and thinking about starting a family, or find yourself pregnant, see your GP as soon as possible.

Going back to education

If you had to put your studies aside for a while because of your illness, there will be a time in your life when you will ask yourself if you are ready to go back to education. It is always best to talk to your doctor or your therapist about this decision. They will be able to advise you how and when you may do it, so you don't jeopardise your recovery.

Some schools or universities may also require you to present a certificate (letter) from your doctor confirming that you are fit to return to your studies.

Retraining

Many people who have been through a mental illness experience a change in their priorities and goals in life. As a consequence, they decide to retrain to change jobs or professions, often in order to make their work/life balance manageable (e.g. less stress, flexible hours enabling taking time off for appointments). It is also not unusual for ex-patients to get involved in supporting others with similar problems.

Case Study

Jane: 'I was working as a quality control technician at a food factory when I started having problems with OCD. I took some time off to recover and when I got better, I came back to my original job. But I quickly realised that due to the nature of my job, keeping my obsessive thoughts and checking urges under control was causing me too much stress. After a chat with my therapist I decided to retrain as a secretary. Now I have a part-time job and I'm working voluntarily as a peer support worker, helping people with mental illness.'

Choosing the course

If you would like to study a particular subject or enrol on a course, check the requirements and ask yourself how this course may be useful to you. You also need to take into consideration if the type of coursework you will be expected to do as this may be affected by your illness. Although, in light of the Disability Discrimination Act, people with mental illness are entitled to equal access to education, the fact that you have a history of OCD may affect your application to some courses. Check with your college or university before you apply.

Studying and mental illness

All universities and colleges have student support and counselling services. Some centres may offer specialist support aimed at people with mental health problems. You may also be entitled to extra time for your assignments, personal support through times of difficulty, or benefits advice, to name a few. Contact your chosen university or college for details.

For more information on studying and mental illness, please see Rethink factsheet at www.rethink.org, click on 'mental health shop' and then browse through the factsheets.

To work or not to work?

There is more to working than just earning money. In addition to income, work provides you with a role in life, structure and purpose to the day, opportunities for social interactions and support. It can be a source of satisfaction, boost your confidence and self-esteem. Some OCD sufferers also see their jobs as a distraction technique, 'time-filler' or even a relapse prevention tool, as well as being busy with productive activities to help keep their mind off disturbing thoughts.

In a nutshell - returning to employment can be an important part of your recovery, if done well and timely.

Whatever your reason for returning to employment, or finding a job whether full or part time, it is important that you do it at the right time, right pace and with a healthy balance. Talk to your doctor or therapist about the best ways of going back to work.

Remember: you may need a certificate from your doctor proving that you are fit for work.

'Returning to employment can be an important part of your recovery, if done well and timely.'

Special programmes

If you live in the UK and have been on any of the incapacity-related benefits you may be entitled to special programmes like Pathways to Work run by Jobcentre Plus, New Deal for Disabled People (available only in certain areas) or Work Preparation Programme. These projects are designed to help people who have been off work for a long time because of sickness or disability.

Ask at your local Jobcentre Plus office or search government websites (e.g. www.direct.gov.uk) for more details and up-to-date information.

Discrimination in the workplace

In the UK, access to employment, education and the provision of good services for people with disabilities, including mental illness are protected by the Disability Discrimination Act, 1995 (DDA). From 1st October 2010 The

Equality Act replaced most of the DDA, providing protection for people with physical and mental disability, as well as for their parents, carers and anyone who has an association with a disabled person. For more information go to www.direct.gov.uk, click on the 'Disabled people' link, then browse the 'Rights and obligations' section.

If you need more information or advice you can also check the Disability Law Service (DLS) website (www.dls.org.uk). DLS is a national charity dedicated to providing information on disability discrimination, employment, education, welfare benefits and other aspects of public and social welfare law to disabled people, their families, carers and advocates.

You can find more information on mental health, education and work on Rethink - the leading national mental health charity's website: www.rethink.org.

Summing Up

Breaking free from your OCD is a great achievement and you should congratulate yourself on that. Don't sit back on your laurels and don't forget what you have learnt during your recovery. In order to remain well you need to 'OCD-proof' your life. A recovery plan with a 'mental health first aid kit' may be helpful in guiding you through the next stages of your recovery and the natural course of your illness. It will come in handy at a time of an 'OCD hiccup' or a more serious relapse.

Remember to keep your life and your relationships healthy and don't be afraid to get a new qualification, a job, a life. Don't be afraid to move on.

Help List

Helplines

ChildLine

NSPCC, Weston House, 42 Curtain Road, London, EC2A 3NH
Tel: 0800 1111 (helpline for children)
Tel: 0 808 800 5000 (helpline for adults concerned about a child)
www.childline.org.uk
Childline is a free helpline for children and young people. It is a confidential, 24/7, counselling service and young people can talk to the staff about any problems they have at home or at school or with drugs, health and well-being.

National Drugs Helpline

Tel: 0800 77 66 00 (helpline)
Text: 82111
www.talktofrank.com
A confidential, 24/7 helpline for people having problems with drugs and advice for their families and friends. Help is available via phone, text and email from the website. The website contains a wealth of useful information about different types of drugs.

NHS Direct

Tel: 0845 46 47
Textphone: 0845 606 4647
www.nhsdirect.nhs.uk
A 24/7 telephone health helpline (England only) providing health advice and reassurance. Also available via textphone.
The website contains a 'Check Your Symptoms' browser. There is also an enquiry form to ask for information not available on the website.

Parentline Plus

CAN Mezzanine, 49-51 East Road, London, N1 6AH
Tel: 0808 800 2222 (helpline)
www.parentlineplus.org.uk
A national charity which works for and with parents. Parentline Plus offers 24/7, confidential telephone support, contact via Skype, live chat, support groups, workshops, local services, courses, online community and more. Email contact form on the website.

Samaritans

Chris, PO Box 9090, Stirling, FK8 2SA
Tel: 08457 90 90 90 (UK)
Tel: 1850 60 90 90 (ROI)
jo@samaritans.org
www.samaritans.org
A confidential, 24/7 service for people in distress, despair or considering suicide.

Health, Mental Health and OCD-Related Resources

Anxiety UK

Zion Community Resource Centre, 339 Stretford Road, Hulme, Manchester, M15 4ZY
Tel: 08444 775 774 (helpline)
www.anxietyuk.org.uk
info@anxiety.uk for general enquiries
A charity dedicated to providing information and support for people living with anxiety through national helpline and dedicated services for members (1:1 therapy services, online support groups and access to specialists).
The website contains information on all types of anxiety disorders, including OCD and BDD, young people and anxiety, as well as advice for family, friends and carers.

A directory of local therapy services and self-help groups and a form for online contact as an alternative to calling the helpline are also available online.

Carers Northern Ireland

58 Howard Street, Belfast, BT1 6PJ
Tel: 028 9043 9843
info@carersni.org
www.carersni.org
Organisation of carers for carers, providing information and advice on carers' rights and support available in Northern Ireland

Carers Scotland

The Cottage, 21 Pearce Street, Glasgow G51 3UT
Tel: 0141 445 3070
info@carersscotland.org
www.carersscotland.org
Organisation of carers for carers in Scotland. Provides information and advice on carers' rights and the support available.

Carers UK

20 Great Dover Steert, London, SE1 4LX
Tel: 020 7378 4999
Advice line: 0808 808 7777 (Wednesday and Thursday 10am-12pm and 2pm-4pm)
info@carersuk.org
adviceline@carersuk.org
www.carersuk.org
Organisation of carers for carers, providing information and advice on carers' rights and support available in England.

Carers Wales

River House, Ynysbridge Court, Gwaelod-y-Garth, Cardiff, CF15 9SS
Tel: 029 2081 1370
info@carerswales.org
www.carerswales.org
Organisation of carers for carers, providing information and advice on carers' rights and support available in Wales.

Disability Law Service

39-45 Calvel Street, London, E1 2BP
Tel: 020 7791 9800 (adviceline, Monday to Friday 10am-5pm)
advice@dls.org.uk
www.dls.org.uk
Organisation which provides advice on benefits, employment, care and
disability discrimination.

GROW

Tel: 1890 474 474 (infoline)
info@grow.ie
www.grow.ie
An Irish support group for people with past or current experience of mental
health problems. The organisation follows 'The12-steps' recovery program and
runs local groups, including special groups for young adults.

Health.com

www.health.com
Website containing information 'with a human touch' on a variety of health
topics, including mental health and OCD.

International OCD Foundation

Office: 112 Water Street, Suite 501, Boston, MA 02109
Mailing address: PO Box 691029, Boston, MA, 02196
Tel: 0617 973 5801
info@ocdfoundation.org
www.ocfoundation.org
International organisation raising awareness of OCD and related disorders,
improving access to resources, supporting research and advocating for the
OCD community.
The website contains information on OCD and related disorders, research and
advice on how to find help. Includes a browser with a 'Find a support group'
option.

Internet Mental Health

www.mentalhealth.com
An American website with information on different mental health problems, medications, stories on recovery and a wealth of useful external links.

Medicinenet.com

www.medicinenet.com
An American online healthcare media publishing company, providing easy-to-read, in-depth medical information.

Mental Health Forum

www.mentalhealthforum.net
An online community for people affected by mental health problems. The site contains a number of fora, covering a wide range of topics, including money, employment, recovery, self-help and support services.

Mental Health Foundation

London Office: 9th Floor, Sea Containers House, 20 Upper Ground, London SE1 9QB
mhf@mhf.org.uk
Scotland Office: Merchants House, 30 George Square, Glasgow, G2 1GE
scotland@mhf.org.uk
Wales Office: Merlin House, No 1 Langstone Business Park, Priory Drive, Newport, NP18 2HJ
walesMHF@mhf.org.uk
www.mentalhealth.org.uk
A UK charity providing information, research and campaigning for people affected by mental health problems. The website contains a mental health A-Z section with information on different mental health problems, treatment options and a list of relevant organisations.

Mental Health Ireland

Mensana House, 6 Adelaide Street, Dun Laoghaire, Co Dublin, Ireland
Tel: (01) 284 11 66
info@mentalhealthireland.ie
www.mentalhealthireland.ie
An Irish voluntary organisation, working through local Mental Health
Associations around the country, campaigning and advocating on mental
health issues, as well as providing information through conferences,
workshops and courses. The website contains a wide range of information
about projects, activities, events, publications and advice on how to get help,
find support, cope with stress, etc.

Mind

England: 15-19 Broadway, Stratford, London E15 4BQ
Wales: 3rd Floor Quebec House, Castlebridge; 5-19 Cowbridge Road East,
Cardiff CF11 9AB
Tel: 0845 766 0163 (infoline)
info@mind.org.uk
www.mind.org.uk
The leading mental health charity for England and Wales, promoting good
mental health for all, providing high quality information and advice, and
campaigning for fair, positive and respectful treatment for people with mental
health problems.

NHS Choices

www.nhs.uk
The online 'front door' to the National Health Services. Provides comprehensive
information on healthy living, numerous health conditions and treatments and
accessing NHS services in England. Also offers a support service for carers
and analysis of health stories in the news.

Northern Ireland Association for Mental Health (NIAMH)

80 University Street, Belfast BT7 1HE
Tel: 028 9032 8474
info@baconwellbeing.org
www.niamh.co.uk

The longest established mental health organisation in Northern Ireland, providing local support throughout Northern Ireland, promoting individual and organisational wellbeing and carrying out research.

OCD Action

Suite 506-509 Davina House; 137-149 Goswell Road, London EC1V 7ET
Tel: 020 7253 5272 (office)
Tel: 0845 390 6232 (helpline, Monday to Friday, 9am-5pm)
support@ocdaction.org.uk
www.ocdaction.org.uk
A UK charity which offers information and support to people affected by OCD over the phone and via email. The website contains a range of information on OCD and related disorders, including advice on self-help, support groups and CBT, and a number of users' fora to share your thoughts and experiences.

OCD Center of Los Angeles

10921 Wilshire Blvd Suite 502, Los Angeles CA 90024; USA
Tel: (+1) 310 335 5443
www.ocdla.com
Private outpatient treatment centre in Los Angeles (USA) dedicated to the treatment of OCD, OCD spectrum disorders and anxiety. The OCDLA website provides a range of information on OCD in adults and young people, OCD spectrum disorders, treatments, a quick OCD test, as well as recommended readings, links and resources.

OCD Ireland

info@ocdireland.org
www.ocdireland.org
An Irish organisation for people with OCD, BDD and trichotillomania. Provides information and support for OCD sufferers, their friends, families, carers, and professionals through support groups and free talks. The website contains a list of scheduled talks and support group meetings, as well as a wealth of information on OCD and related disorders, treatments, links, self-help book reviews and advice on finding a therapist.

OCDkids

www.ocdkids.org
OCD-UK website for children; contains easy-to-understand information on the disorder and treatment.

OCD Support Group Christchurch, New Zealand

Floor 2, Securities House, 221 Gloucester Street, 8011, Christchurch, New Zealand
Tel: (+64) 03 377 9665
www.ocd.org.nz
A New Zealand website providing the latest news on OCD, as well as information on the disorder, treatments available and a personal experience section.

OCD-UK

PO Box 8955, Nottingham NG10 9AU, UK
Tel: 0845 120 3778
admin@ocduk.org
www.ocduk.org
The leading UK charity working for and with OCD sufferers. The website contains comprehensive information on different types and aspects of OCD and related disorders, including easy-to-read leaflets for young people, advice for family and friends, recommended readings, guidance on self-help. There is also a directory of support and self-help groups in England, Scotland, Wales, Northern Ireland and Ireland and discussion fora.

Patient UK

www.patient.co.uk
Website with a lot of information about health, lifestyle, diseases, medicines; as well as directories linking to UK health websites, support groups, information for carers and other relevant resources.

PsychNet-UK

Tel: 0845 122 8622 (counselling line, Monday - Friday 10am-1pm & 7pm - 10pm)
www.psychnet-uk.com

A website developed for mental health professionals and those interested in mental health practices, listing information and links to mental health and psychology articles, chat rooms, blogs, advice, etc. It also provides a confidential telephone counselling service.

SANE

1st Floor Cityside House, 40 Adler Steert, London E1 1EE
Tel: 0845 767 8000 (SANEline - out-of-hours confidential telephone support and information for people affected by mental health problems)
sanemail@sane.org.uk (support via email)
www.sane.org.uk
SANE provides support and information for people suffering from mental health problems, their families and carers over the telephone (SANEline) and via email (SANEmail)

Stuck in a Doorway

www.stuckinadoorway.org
An Internet site for people affected by OCD, with a number of OCD-related online fora and members from over 200 countries.

The Black Dog

www.theblackdog.net
Ireland's interactive self-help site for men, providing information on health, including mental wellbeing.

Professional Organisations

British Association for Behavioural and Cognitive Psychotherapies (BABCP)

Imperial House, Hornby Street, Bury, BL9 5BN
Tel: 0161 705 4304
babcp@babcp.com
www.babcp.com

BABCP is a leading organisation for cognitive behavioural therapy (CBT) in the UK, providing accreditation recognised by healthcare providers, training institutions and some health insurance companies. The website enables you to search for a therapist by their name, area, second language spoken or by the condition they provide treatment for.

British Association of Counselling and Psychotherapists

BACP House, 15 St John's Business Park, Lutterworth, Leicestershire, LE17 4HB
Tel: 014 55 88 3300 (general enquiries)
Text: 014 55 550243
bacp@bacp.co.uk
www.bacp.co.uk
A professional body for counsellors and psychotherapists which sets standards for practice and training and participates in the development of counselling and psychotherapy at an international level. The members' register can be searched for a therapist by the name, region, services or special interests.

Irish Association for Counselling and Psychotherapy

21 Dublin Road, Bray, County Wicklow, Ireland
Tel: (+353) 1 27 23 427
iacp@iacp.ie
www.irish-counselling.ie
An Irish organisation which develops and maintains professional standards in psychotherapy and counselling, representing interests of clients and practitioners. IACP provides a telephone referral and information service and an online directory for psychotherapists, counsellors and supervisors

Irish Council for Psychotherapy

73 Quinns Road, Shankin, County Doublin, Ireland
Tel: (+353) 1 272 2105
www.psychotherapy-ireland.com

An Irish organisation, which promotes and maintains standards of care, training and professional conduct among psychotherapists. The Council maintains a register of its members and provides a 'Find a Psychotherapist' service on the website.

The Royal College of Psychiatrists

17 Belgrave Square; London SW1X 8PG
Tel: 020 7235 2351
reception@rcpsych.ac.uk
www.rcpsych.ac.uk
The professional and educational body for psychiatrists in the UK. The website contains a wealth of information on different aspects of mental health problems, including easy-to-read and up-to-date information on a range of mental health conditions with treatments explained in 20 languages and advice on how to get help.

The College of Psychiatry of Ireland

5 Herbert Street, Dublin 2, Ireland
Tel: (01) 661 8450
info@irishpsychiatry.ie
www.irishpsychiatry.ie
The professional, training and educational body for psychiatrists in Ireland. The website contains resources with information on mental health problems and available treatments, advice on how psychiatric services in Ireland work, how to seek help and a list of useful, Irish support websites.

UK Council for Psychotherapy

2nd Floor, Edward House, 2 Wakley Street, London, EC1V 7LT
Tel: 020 7014 99 55
info@ukcp.org.uk
www.psychotherapy.org.uk
A voluntary regulatory body for psychotherapists in the UK; also provides information on using psychotherapy, explaining different types of psychotherapy and their merits. UKCP maintains a register of psychotherapists, which can be searched using the 'Find a Therapist' section on the website.

Glossary

Antibodies
Proteins produced by the immune system to identify and neutralise bacteria, viruses and other foreign substances and organisms in the blood system.

Antipsychotics
Drugs used to treat different types of psychosis; some of them also have anti-anxiety properties.

Anxiolytics
Drugs that relieve anxiety. The most common anxiolytics are benzodiazepines and SSRIs. Some anti-psychotic drugs can also reduce anxiety and therefore may be used for this purpose.

Benzodiazepines
A class of anxiolytic drugs which includes lorazepam (Ativan), clonazepam, diazepam (Valium), chlordiazepoxine and alprazolam (Xanax). These medications are indicated for the short-term relief of acute anxiety and should not be used long term due to their addictive potential.

Body Dysmorphic Disorder (BDD/Dysmorphophobia)
An anxiety disorder in which the sufferer is preoccupied with an imagined or minor defect in their appearance. These obsessions can be related to any body part, but most commonly to perceived or slight flaws of the person's face, thinning hair, acne, asymmetry or disproportion of body features (e.g. breasts, genitals, feet, etc.). Sometimes the complaints are vague and focused on perceived generalised ugliness. In severe cases these beliefs are so fixed and firm that they reach the level of delusions.

Child and Adolescent Mental Health Team/Service (CAMHT/S)
A multidisciplinary team or service for children and adolescents; similar in role and structure to CMHT.

Cognitive Behavioural Therapy (CBT)

A psychotherapeutic approach based on the concept that the way we think about things affects how we feel and behave. It is a relatively short term, very structured therapy that focuses on the present. It helps the person learn to understand the connection between their thoughts, emotions and behaviours and change the negative, maladaptive patterns.

There is a lot of evidence that the CBT approach is effective in a range of mental health problems, including depression, anxiety and OCD.

Cognitive Therapy

A form of psychotherapy, which focuses on dysfunctional thinking, e.g. all-or-nothing thinking, over-generalisation or selective perception. During the therapy the person learns to recognise these patterns and is encouraged to change them.

Community Mental Health Team (CMHT)

A multidisciplinary team of various mental health professionals, usually comprising of community psychiatric nurses, social workers, occupational therapists, psychologists, psychiatrists, community support workers etc. CMHTs usually provide specialist services for people with severe and enduring mental illness.

Community Psychiatric Nurse (CPN)

A nurse specialising in mental health. Many CPNs have additional therapeutic skills and some train to become fully qualified therapists (e.g. in CBT).

Comorbid

A problem or illness co-existing, but not related to, another health problem.

Compulsions

Repetitive acts or behaviours which the person feels forced to carry out, even if they know it's irrational. Attempts to resist these urges cause anxiety. Compulsions are carried out in response to obsessive thoughts in order to prevent worry or lessen anxiety. However, the relief they bring is only temporary. Compulsive rituals are often accompanied by doubts that the behaviours have not been executed properly which leads to further repetitions.

Counselling

A psychological approach focused on facilitating emotional acceptance, personal growth and a better understanding in order to help the person live a more satisfying life. The issues discussed during the sessions can vary according to the person's needs and may be related to problems from childhood, relationship difficulties, making specific decisions or dealing with loss.

Exposure and Response Prevention (ERP)

A form of cognitive behaviour therapy effective in OCD. ERP is based on the process of habituation - the ability of our nervous system to 'get used to' a stimulus through repeated, prolonged contact. The idea is to reduce anxiety and discomfort associated with OCD symptoms by exposing the sufferer to their obsessions. Exposure to obsessions is done in small steps. Habituation provides 'emotional numbness' to the situation, which provokes intensive feelings of anxiety and fear.
The ultimate goal is complete habituation ('numbness') to the feared situation or object in mind.

Habit Reversal Training

A behavioural therapy effective in reducing tics, compulsive skin-picking, trichotillomania and other impulse control disorders.

Immune system

Body defence system consisting of several elements and complex processes, involving special cells and proteins (antibodies).

Obsessions

Persistent, unpleasant, intrusive images, ideas or thoughts, which keep coming into the person's mind, despite efforts to resist them. Although these thoughts are perceived as own, they are disturbing and unpleasant and cause a lot of anxiety.

Obsessive-compulsive disorder (OCD)

A mental disorder characterised by persistent, unwanted, unpleasant thoughts (obsessions), provoking anxiety; and repetitive, irrational urges to carry out acts (compulsions) aimed at reducing the anxiety or neutralising the obsessive thought.

Obsessive Compulsive Personality Disorder (OCPD)

Also known as anankastic personality disorder – is a type of personality disorder characterised by preoccupations with details, rules, lists; in general - order. People who have this type of personality are organised perfectionists, with great attention to detail. They are usually cautious, prefer routine, predictability and repetition, and struggle with anything which is not black-or-white. These traits develop through adolescence and early adulthood and are part of their personality, being 'in harmony' with the person, even if their family, friends or work colleagues see them as problematic.

Occupational Therapist (OT)

A mental health professional who uses purposeful, daily living activities and interventions based on art, exercise and occupational skills to promote recovery and regain vocational potential. Many mental health OTs develop therapeutic skills and often run groups (e.g. anxiety or depression management) or even individual therapy.

National Institute for Health and Clinical Excellence (NICE)

NICE is an independent organisation responsible for providing guidelines on promoting good health, prevention and treatment for various health conditions in England and Wales. The guidelines are developed, reviewed and updated regularly and provide recommendations for most appropriate treatment regimes.

Neurotransmitter

A brain chemical; substance produced and released by brain cells in order to transmit nerve impulses from one cell to another. Neurotransmitters act as communication between brain cells. There are several types of neurotransmitters.

Psychoanalysis

A psychotherapeutic approach developed by Sigmund Freud. Psychoanalysis involves the exploration of the person's unconscious thought processes to find the causes for certain symptoms and areas of resistance which block emotional growth and prevent changes. Psychoanalysis is a long-term and intensive form of therapy. This is the first psychological approach that was developed in late 19th century and has laid foundations for the multitude of talking therapies.

Psychoanalysis is still used, but its application has changed and it is not as popular as it has been in the past.

Psychodynamic Therapy

A psychotherapy approach which developed from psychoanalysis and is based on similar theories but is usually less intensive and shorter term.

Psychological approaches

See talking therapies.

Psychosis (psychotic illness, psychotic disorder)

A mental disorder where people develop unusual beliefs (delusions) or can see, hear or smell things that are not there (hallucinations). Psychosis is a very generic term and often used as a 'temporary' diagnosis before the more accurate is reached.

In some type of psychosis the sufferer's thoughts are disorganised, like in schizophrenia. Psychosis can also have a strong mood component with elevated or lowered mood.

Psychotherapist (therapist)

A mental health professional who pursued special training in one or more types of psychotherapy. In the UK, psychotherapists are often psychologists, CPNs, OTs, or psychiatrists by background.

Pure Obsessions (Pure O)

Purely Obsessional OCD is a type of OCD in which the sufferer experiences obsessive thoughts, but their compulsive behaviours are not visible. It is because the anxiety-reducing act is performed in the sufferer's mind, e.g. an intrusive image of running in front of a car is 'neutralised' by counting to a preferred number or saying a mantra/prayer.

Relapse

Return of a disease after a period of wellness (remission).

Ritual

In a medical sense a detailed act, procedure or a series of acts carried out to relieve anxiety.

Schizophrenia

Severe mental illness where people develop unusual beliefs (delusions) or can see, hear or smell things that are not there (hallucinations). Schizophrenia often also affects thinking and emotions which results in disorganised thoughts and social withdrawal.

There are different sub-types of schizophrenia (paranoid, catatonic, disorganised, undifferentiated, residual), depending on which symptoms dominate in the clinical picture. Schizophrenia is a psychotic disorder.

Selective Serotonin Reuptake Inhibitors (SSRIs)

Medication which increases the amount of a brain chemical (neurotransmitter), called serotonin, in your brain by blocking the process of reuptake of serotonin released by the brain cells. The process results in more active serotonin available for brain cells.

SSRIs have been found effective in a range of mental health problems, particularly depression, anxiety and OCD.

Serotonin

A neurotransmitter involved in the processes underlying depression, anxiety disorders, OCD and many others.

Serotonin Reuptake Inhibitors (SRIs)

Medication which also increases the amount of serotonin in your brain by blocking the process of reuptake and working also on other brain chemicals. This group of medications includes SSRIs and other antidepressants. SRIs have been found to be effective in a range of mental health problems including depression, anxiety and OCD.

Talking therapies (psychological therapies, psychological approaches)

Popular name for psychotherapy derived from the fact that these interventions involve talking about thoughts, emotions and feelings.

Tic

An involuntary, compulsive, repetitive and stereotyped movement (spasm) or a sound.

Tricyclics

A class of antidepressants deriving their name from their chemical structure (three rings); this is the first discovered class of antidepressants, effective but with a range of potential side effects. They are still used, although rarely, in depression, anxiety, OCD and treatment of pain.

Tourette's Syndrome

An inherited nervous system disorder characterised by different types of tics.

References

AnxietyUK [Online] Available at: http://www.anxietyuk.org.uk/ [accessed on 10 November 2010]

Directgov. Public services in one place [Online]. Available at: http://www.direct.gov.uk [accessed on 1 November 2010]

Gelder M, Mayou & R, Geddes J (1999) Psychiatry. Oxford University Press

Hyman, BM, Pedrick C. (2005) The OCD workbook: your guide to breaking free from obsessive-compulsive disorder. New Harbinger Publications.

National Collaborative Centre for Mental Health (2006) Obessive-compulsive disorder: core interventions in the treatments of obsessive-compulsive disorder and body dysmorphic disorder. National Clinical Practice Guideline Number 31. The British Psychological Society and The Royal College of Psychiatrist [Online]. Available at: http://guidance.nice.org.uk/CG31/Guidance/pdf/English [Accessed 30 October 2010].

OCD-UK. [online] Available at: http://www.ocduk.org/ [Accessed 10 November 2010]

Rethink. [Online] Available at: http://www.rethink.org/ [accessed on 1 November 2010]

Scott, K M et al. (2010) Gender and the relationship between marital status and first onset of mood, anxiety and substance use disorders, Psychological Medicine, 2010, vol. 40, issue 09, http://journals.cambridge.org/action/display Abstract?fromPage=online&aid=7863174, accessed 9 January 2011.

The Royal College of Psychiatrist (2007) obsessive-compulsive disorder. [online] available at: http://www.rcpsych.ac.uk/mentalhealthinfoforall/problems/obsessivecompulsivedisorder/obsessivecomplusivedisorder.aspx [Accessed 30 October 2010]

Wegner DM et al. (1987) Paradoxical effects of thought suppression. JPSP, 53, 636-647 [online] Available at: http://faculty.babson.edu/krollag/org_site/soc_psych/wegner_tho_sup.html] [Accessed on 25 January 2011].

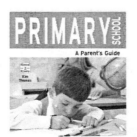

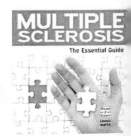